EMBRACING
INFINITE
POSSIBILITIES

EMBRACING
INFINITE
POSSIBILITIES

LETTING GO
OF FEAR
TO FIND YOUR
HIGHEST POTENTIAL

DR. BERNARD A. HARRIS JR.

SAVIO
REPVBLIC

A SAVIO REPUBLIC BOOK
An Imprint of Post Hill Press
ISBN: 979-8-88845-743-6
ISBN (eBook): 979-8-88845-744-3

Embracing Infinite Possibilities:
Letting Go of Fear to Find Your Highest Potential
© 2025 by Dr. Bernard A. Harris Jr.
All Rights Reserved

Cover Design by Cody Corcoran

posthillpress.com
New York • Nashville
Published in the United States of America

1 2 3 4 5 6 7 8 9 10

CONTENTS

FOREWORD

My first book was *Dream Walker: A Journey of Achievement and Inspiration*, an autobiographical account of my life. When I initially conceived the concept for a book, it was my intent to write something that people would enjoy and, more importantly, use as a resource for inspiration. In discussions with the publisher and editor, they encouraged me to begin my journey as an author by writing an autobiography. So, I did. The reception for the book was wonderful. In general, people enjoyed my story. I appreciated all the words of praise and encouragement. One such example was a young man who said that my story was an inspiration to him and inspired him to chart a new course for his life. It expanded his mind to the possibilities and aspirations in life.

One of my lifelong goals is to instill inspiration as well as aspiration in people. Accordingly, this book looks to build on the first book by serving as a roadmap to discover the power within each of us. Recently, I re-read *The Secret* by Rhonda Byrne and discovered that the power that I used to achieve was the same power that they and their colleagues wrote about. Indeed, this power is not a secret but a law that enables all who desire to take advantage of the one force that binds us all.[1]

---

[1]   Byrne, Rhonda, *The Secret*, Atria Books, 2007.

If we are students of the universe, it is clear to me that each of us must find this power within to find our own way and in our own time—some through the experiences of life, some by reading, others by observing, being taught, or through self-study. I encourage you to find your own path. The hope of this book, as the companion to my first, will open your mind to the infinite possibilities of life.

In *Living the Life of Your Dreams: The Secret to Turning Your Dreams into Reality*, my good friend Marilyn Tam captured the key elements to discovering and fulfilling your dreams. She says, "You have a choice; you can live the life that you've dreamed of living."[2] She is absolutely right. At some point in your life, you must decide that you want to live the life of your dreams. You must choose! No one can make you dream or tell you what to dream. I know that many will try but a dream only becomes reality when it truly comes from you. And in doing so, you set the stage for making your dream a reality.

"Dreams are the reality of the future."

Your dreams, your future.

I have a dear friend who has struggled with this all their life. They would let others around them define their reality. As a result, they are in a constant tug of war with themselves and those they valued. By accepting their path for them, they gave up the opportunity to live a fulfilled life. As a consequence, they live in doubt every day. You cannot let others define you. Otherwise, you would always be thinking—What should I do? What should I wear? What would people think of me? Should I join this group or that, to fit in and/or to be accepted?

---

[2]   Tam, Marilyn, *Living the Life of Your Dreams: The Secrets to Turning Your Dreams into Reality*, Waterside, 2011.

All of us have had these issues to deal with at some point in our lives. Liberation comes when you discover just how unimportant these external things really are. When you reach this point, you will no longer see the world around you as hostile and unforgiving. In this reality, you will be free to be who you really are. There is great power with this realization! This self-endowed power releases you from the burden of self-doubt. There is no greater power in the world, except that of God. This is, in fact, the truth that God wants for each of us—the realization of our own strength that we are an integral part of something greater than ourselves. I call that "Universe" or GOD.

The question is, if you are the one caught in the middle of this personal crisis, how do you escape these feelings of doubt? How do you get out of this never-ending spiral of despair, which in extreme cases can sometimes lead to death? Indeed, for some people, this crisis can lead to depression and even suicide. When we encounter individuals like this, we must practice great patience, simply listen, and get them professional help as soon as possible. For most of us, though, we simply struggle with the constant issues that arise throughout our life. And we somehow manage through them.

To be lost without direction is a miserable existence. That is why knowing who you are and what or who you want to be is so critical. When I am in conversations with people struggling, they usually ask: What do you think I should do? We have all had these conversations.

I would love to say that I can only imagine how that feels. But if I am honest, I have to admit that I have been in a similar place at different times in my life, too. I believe we all have experienced periods in our lives where we have gotten depressed about something. The million-dollar questions are: How do you get out of the sprawling circle of conformity and its conse-quences? How do you get out of ambivalence and into knowing? This behavior never leads to lasting peace. If you conform to what others want versus what is right for you, you'll struggle to get where you truly wish to go. Lasting peace comes from within yourself, never from external sources.

Life always has a way of testing us. Just when we think things are going well, in comes change and sometimes disappointment. It is during these times that we must rely on our inner strength to carry us through. And when we falter, as we all sometimes do, turning to a higher power can make the difference. My strength comes through my faith in God.

My desire in sharing my journey is for you to find some aspects that will help you in your own life. I present an honest discussion of my struggles, ambitions, hopes, and dreams as a testimony to the voyage that we all face. In doing so, I hope it provides a guidepost for you.

CHAPTER 1

UNDERSTAND YOUR PLACE IN THE WORLD

....

*"If you do not know your place in the world
and the meaning of your life, you should know
there is something to blame; and it is not the
social system, or your intellect, but the way
in which you have directed your intellect."*
—Leo Tolstoy

....

On February 9, 1995, I stepped out of the comfort of the Space Shuttle Discovery's airlock and into the history books as the first African American to walk in space. Looking back on the experience, it was a tremendous honor for me to represent a group of people who had once been slaves in the United States—the same country whose name was emblazoned on Discovery's hull and whose flag was on a shoulder patch of my spacesuit.

At the time, though, I wasn't truly aware of the significance that this represented to people and to the nation. I was only fulfilling a boyhood dream of following in the footsteps of two great men to whom I looked up. When Neil Armstrong and

Buzz Aldrin set foot on the moon in 1969, I was only thirteen, staring at a black and white television and sharing the dream of millions of American kids that day—of leaving this planet and traveling to other worlds.

My dreams of visiting other planets weren't fueled purely by the spirit of adventure. The realities of the day forced me to acknowledge that I was living in a country that at the time thought very little of its Black citizens. After all, on that very same black and white TV on most days, I could see my fellow Blacks being persecuted by white Americans at all levels. But that didn't deter me because my heart and mind were set. If I had anything to do with it, my dreams would not be deferred.

Part of that dream came to life that day in February 1995. I was payload commander on the first flight of the new joint Russian-American Space Program on Space Shuttle Discovery STS-63. The mission highlights included the first rendezvous with the Russian Space Station Mir, conducting more than forty-eight scientific investigations in the SpaceHab module, and the deployment and retrieval of Spartan 204 satellite. I walked in space during the extravehicular activity (EVA) that tested new thermal protection devices for the spacesuits, used a new electronic EVA checklist, conducted mass handling of the 3,000-pound Spartan satellite, and evaluated EVA tools in preparation for the construction of the International Space Station (ISS). On that mission, I logged 198 hours, 29 minutes, 129 orbits, and 2.9 million miles in space.

Still, I had my share of nerves. As I floated out of the hatch into the vastness of space, I remember being both excited but scared to death at the possibility that things could go wrong. Fortunately, my mind and courage prevailed, and we worked for a full six hours carrying out the objectives of the mission. By all accounts, it was a successful venture for myself and my EVA partner, Michael Foale, two neophytes to space walking.

At the end of our task, I had about an hour to absorb what I had accomplished and simply take it all in. After all, only a few have had the opportunity to do what I had done. I was unique, exceptional, an example of bravery, and an American hero. So, I thought.

But the experience meant much more than a stream of self-congratulation.

As remarkable an accomplishment as that was, an even greater realization occurred—I had a chance to look upon our planet, from space. A God's eye view like no other! Many astronauts have experienced a similar revelation—a sense of connection between themselves and the blue ball spinning in front of them. In that moment, my belief in a higher power was reaffirmed. I could feel it within me. I had found a new view, a new perspective that would change my life and my mission. In those moments, I recognized my place in the universe.

You may never have the opportunity for an epiphany in an airless, zero-gravity environment. But that doesn't mean you can't have precisely the same sort of experience, no matter where you happen to be.

I'm going to help you get there.

FINDING YOUR PLACE IN THE WORLD–WHY NOW?

If the idea of taking the time to discover your true place in the world appeals to you—perhaps for the first time in your life— you're not alone.

I started to write this book when we were finally emerging from the Covid-19 pandemic, more than two years fraught with anxiety and isolation exacerbated at times by dishonesty and ineptitude at the very highest levels of our government. It's been harrowing, to say the least.

But, like everything, there have been positives. One bit of good news is that the fear and uncertainty of the pandemic have prompted many of us to look inside ourselves—to work to truly understand who we are and what is of value to us. We're beginning to seriously consider how we work, play, and live with others. Moreover, it's happening to people at all ages, from boomers and Gen X, to Gen Y and Gen Z or, as I call them, the lucky ones who begin this invaluable journey early in their lives.

As it happened, my journey toward enlightenment began when I was six with my parents' divorce. It seems odd to say it, but it's true. My family's break-up was my first life trial. That event changed my life in ways that have been far reaching, many that you will hear about in this book. It includes our move to the Navajo Nation in Arizona.

When I was not playing with my friends, I used to sit on the front sidewalk of our apartment in Greasewood, Arizona, just staring out at the beautiful landscape. My mother had moved there to take a job as a teacher for the Bureau of Indian Affairs (BIA). It was a very interesting place for a kid from Texas to grow up in—it was probably the primary reason I began to ask what an older, more mature person might refer to as critical life questions. Still, it started with the sorts of issues that any child might raise:

- What are we doing here?
- Why did my mother have to be here?
- Why did she take this job?

- Why did we, the children, have to come?
- What does our future hold?
- And the most important one: Who am I and who would I become?

Beginning with those basic questions, I started to get to know myself. As a Black kid in this strange land of Native Americans, I was literally and figuratively surrounded by people who were completely different from me. Although others came later, we were the only Black family at first, so I came to understand that I had to rely on myself. The only way to survive was to find my inner strength.

It wasn't easy by any means. I was teased about the texture of my hair and the color of my skin. One day, shortly after starting elementary school, I was just standing alone on the playground, and the kids looked at me, laughed, and ran up behind me to quickly touch my hair. I didn't understand the language, but I understood that I was different and strange to them. The same was true for me. I had never seen a Native American. I felt very isolated initially. The teasing helped me accept that I was alone in many ways and that I would have to become stronger. But I needed to figure out how to get stronger without physically fighting all the time. Over time, they eventually accepted me and my siblings.

It all turned out rather well. As kids do, we found a way to communicate beyond words—with deeds. I began to explore the world around me with my newfound friends. I learned of their customs and beliefs. More importantly, I began to understand them and they me. Indeed, those were the best of times and the worst of times for this little boy to navigate.

Still, despite how others tried to make me feel, I knew that I was more. In many ways, I felt I was better than those who taunted me. Looking back, I don't believe that my plight was any different from other kids at that age. In that sense, I wasn't alone. There were—and still are—countless children in this country picked on for being different. But what I discovered was that I was stronger than I had initially given myself credit for. Calling my worth into question strengthened me without my even knowing it. I began to look deeply into myself for inner strength so as not to fall victim to my surroundings. I was learning to accept who I was, despite what others may have thought of me.

A few years later, as I was sitting out on that sidewalk outside our one-bedroom apartment, I began to dig deeper, weighing the question of who I was. I remember staring at my hand, examining every detail—the length of my fingers, the color of my skin, the lines of my palm. As I looked at my hand within the landscape surrounding me, I started to gain some perspective of who I was in respect to the world around me.

Our apartment looked out onto a valley below, with mountains as the backdrop. I had done these many times before; sitting there at different times of the day was inspiring. The sun's light would change the scenery, creating different colors and images from the shadows, depending on the time of day. I was mesmerized by the hues of reds, blues, and purple with streaks of gold. It was absolutely beautiful! (For those who have been to the Grand Canyon, you might have experienced something similar. In fact, where we lived was only 200 miles from Greasewood, Arizona.)

I realize that it was a rather deep thought for a ten-year-old to have. But I guess I have always been a little different in that way. It helped me discover one singular attribute that has stayed with me my entire life. I am inquisitive. I like to examine things in detail, including myself. I wanted to know how things worked. I constantly asked questions—What? Why? How? Some might say that these were the early signs of a scientist. Probably.

And, in trying to figure out my place in the world, I also discovered my spiritual side.

There was only one church in our community. My mother was a very religious woman who wanted their children to know God as she did, so she forced us to go to church every Sunday. My brother, sister, and I were not thrilled about giving up perfectly good play time to sit in a church pew. But one Sunday, something truly amazing took place. The minister made a remark that struck a chord with me. I can't remember precisely what it was but, for the very first time, I sat up and began to listen.

He talked about the concept of a higher being, which he called God. At the end of his sermon, he asked people to come forward if they wanted to know God. The next thing I knew, I was up at the front of the church. I was scared. I had no idea what to expect. But I was up there, nonetheless. And I "accepted God" into my life in front of my family and all present there. For those who are Christians, "accepting God" is the entry ticket to salvation.

I remember vividly what happened next. Following the service, the minister took me into his office for a prayer. As we knelt and he prayed, I looked up at the minister and out the window behind him. I saw the spirit of God permeating the window in the form of beautiful, vibrant sunlight.

In that moment, I knew God existed, a discovery that would direct my actions and thoughts for the rest on my life. I felt that God was real and that one of my goals would be to explore a relationship with this universal source.

That was an enormous step of self-discovery, of figuring out my place in the universe. I needed to spend time with myself to do that, something that many people don't do. Why? Some of us may be afraid of what we might discover. Some of us are simply uncomfortable being alone and we look outside ourselves for support and validation. But spending time alone with oneself helps you discover your place in the world. If you don't, you can fall victim to external influence.

That makes me think of actors. Their professional success depends on how they capture the role of other people. I have heard some say that they are happiest when they're in character. But some also struggle with being themselves, living in the real world and coping with real issues and problems. There are many examples of actors who illustrate this, one being Philip Seymour Hoffman who died of a drug overdose. Hoffman's death was officially ruled an accident caused by "acute mixed drug intoxication, including heroin, cocaine, benzodiazepines, and amphetamine."[3] Recently, I also watched a documentary on the life of Whitney Houston called *Can I Be Me*.[4] It told her story, the good and the bad. It highlighted her struggles with the pressures of being famous and its cost to her soul. In both of these examples, their struggles ultimately resulted in death.

When I read accounts of their lives, I can't help but wonder why. Why does this happen to even the most talented of us? The reality is that I do not know the details of their struggles. They were brilliant artists, and their talents will be missed.

---

[3]   "Philip Seymour Hoffman Died from Drugs Mix." Sky News. Archived on August 23, 2016. Retrieved February 28, 2014.

[4]   Felsenthal, Julia, "*Whitney: Can I Be Me* Is a Tale of Two Whitney Houstons," *Vogue*, August 24, 2017, https://www.vogue.com/article/whitney-houston-can-i-be-me-showtime-documentary.

It's essential to know who you are and what motivates you, while working to keep things in perspective. I know firsthand how this feels. Honestly, I have been in a similar place at different times in my life—not as extreme, but exhausting and discouraging, nonetheless. We all experience periods in our lives when we become depressed. The question is how to get out of the sprawling circle of conformity and its consequences. If you conform to what others want versus what is right for you, you'll inevitably struggle. Lasting peace comes from within yourself, never from external sources. In the case of Whitney Houston, she simply longed to be herself. The key is to know yourself as much as you can, so when faced with a challenge or problem, you can remain true to yourself before the situation swallows you up. It can literally save your life.

This isn't an issue just with former astronauts and world-famous actors and entertainers. Prior to giving a speech to a group of educators about my life and mission, the person who would introduce me asked what it was like in outer space. After I answered, I asked them what they did for a living.

"I'm a teacher. My job isn't nearly as important as yours," they replied with obvious sincerity.

"Are you kidding me?" I had to lower my voice to mask the shock in my tone. "Your profession is the most important of all! What you do is the foundation of this nation. As an educator, you hold the key to our nation's success. This country's educational system in many communities is in disarray! High-quality teachers and educators are the only hope for this nation's students and ultimately for the continued leadership of America. This is how important your job is!"

I guess I had started my speech sooner than I expected. Still, it was clear that their doubts and misgivings had nothing to do with the profession. They had everything to do with their feelings about themselves.

Again, they're not alone. Too many of us have doubts about ourselves. We constantly find fault in ourselves and others in an attempt to convince us of the validity of our existence. I, too, had doubts about my abilities and the choices that I have made at different points in my life. It's just part of being human.

When I was eleven, my mother married a man who would become my father, even though he was technically my stepfather. He was a police officer and a proud Black man. I learned a great deal from him through the years. He taught me how to be a man. But there was one thing that my stepfather did that I didn't like; he teased me about being a "scaredy-cat." I was an introvert and a quiet person, someone who needed time to think and contemplate things. He mistook my caution as fear. But what he didn't misconstrue was my doubt in myself. How could I not doubt myself, given how the world saw me as a "little colored boy," with a limited future? The stereotypes in the sixties were all around me. It tinted how I saw myself. So, I had doubts about my legitimacy, colored by the perspective of the outside world. In his own way, he was trying to toughen me up for that world that I was about to face.

The challenge—and damage—comes when we cannot overcome these doubts. That's when we can become lost. By taking the time to truly know ourselves, we can grow through trials and tribulations, instead of drowning in the pain and discontent of the moment.

WE ARE NOT WHO PEOPLE THINK WE ARE

I was in medical school in the early eighties, during a time of affirmative action. Emerging from the sixties and seventies, the consciousness of the nation had shifted to trying to be more inclusive. So, there was an initiative to address the racial disparities of this country—what we call the affirmative action programs. One strategy was to establish quotas in colleges and universities with the objective of diversifying enrollment.

During this period, many Black and Brown students were accepted into institutions that previously rejected them. I was one of those students. At the end of my education at the University of Houston, I applied to medical school. I had excellent grades, top recommendations from faculty, and a healthy dose of ambition, but after applying to six schools, only one accepted me—the Texas Tech University School of Medicine. So, I ventured out to west Texas to a community that was known for growing cotton. In fact, a generation of Black people lived there because they had come to support the cotton industry.

On the first day of class, I realized I was the only Black among sixty students. Moreover, there were only two other Black students in the entire school. To add to the complexity of the situation, it was a newly chartered school and there were doubts at the time about how long the school itself would survive. (Things have dramatically changed; it now has approximately 200 students per class, has diversified its enrollment, and is one of the leading medical institutions in the country.)

The perception of me and others like me was that we only got into the school because of the color of our skin. Nothing could have been further from the truth. We were there because we worked twice as hard to become part of a system that was not particularly supportive of us, despite outward appearances.

(In fact, there were some schools that measured their quality by high rejection rates: "*See, we told you that you weren't qualified to be here.*")

There are many stories of young men and women who didn't make it through the system, not because they weren't qualified, but because of the racism they faced. They are the forgotten ones, rejected and cast out because of the color of their skin.

I was determined that this would not happen to me. So, I hunkered down, studied harder, and kept my faith despite all that seemed to oppose me. I had to find my place in an insecure world.

SINS OF THE FATHER

I woke up one morning from a dream of loss. I don't remember the details of the dream, only that it involved my father and a great sense of missing him.

Since the divorce of my parents, I have felt this way, and I have hidden it all my life. Sure, my mother remarried when I was eleven and my stepfather did the best that he could. But there remains this void where my father should have been. I still see those two little boys on the sofa of my grandmother's house in Temple, Texas after my mother's escape from the misery of her marriage, and I feel sad. I was also disappointed that despite my father's promises to get us all back together, it never happened. I have had this hole in my heart and soul ever since.

As I now look back at my life, I am struck by the impact this moment had on me as an individual...both positive and negative. On the negative side, it is simply not having his love and presence in my life, a hole that was left when a father's love wasn't present. Despite how I might justify the loss, having someone who loves you unconditionally, who is there when you fall, a person to share your ups and downs with, is extremely important. Most importantly, it is also crucial for a child to have a father whom you can look up to and emulate, someone who can serve as a construct of your role as a man. I missed all that.

On the positive side, I left behind the emotional stress of the marriage and my father's own personal struggles and baggage. As a young man growing up in a poor inner-city neighborhood in Philadelphia, he had many problems and challenges. In many respects, he did not receive the very thing that I was looking for from him. It is sometimes funny how life repeats itself. Back then, there was no such thing as being self-aware. You simply toughed it out and lived your life. He did not have the insight or wisdom to figure out his stuff. So, how could I expect that he would have the tools to be a good father?

As I became more aware, I developed behaviors that prepared me to succeed despite this missing piece of the equation in my life. With the help of my mother and family, I created a persona of strength and competence, which became my foundation for achievement. At some level, I wasn't going to be like my father. Where he failed, I achieved. My lack became abundance in different ways and aspects of my life. My goal was to become a super father and a super man. The result created this person who used achievement as the construct for success in all things—a drive to become all that I could be.

I cannot tell you how many times during an introduction of me before a speech, where I sit there listening to all the accolades, and I wonder to myself, "Who is that guy they are talking about?" I have overcompensated because of this drive to be different…to be better…to be perfect. It has taken a lot of counseling to get to this point, where I realized that I am trying to fill an empty space that can never be filled, and I am learning to acknowledge and accept it.

INSECURITY

Of course, many of the challenges facing you in finding your place in the world have everything to do with insecurities of all sorts. Understanding and working to overcome them are key to getting to know who you are.

One of the most difficult things I have done is to manage people in my business—personalities to deal with, hidden agendas, differences in motivations and desires. I will be the first to admit this is not my strength. I am a motivator. A visionary and a dreamer, yes, but not a manager of people. I am admittedly insecure when I have to take on the sorts of issues that fall into your lap when directing other people. While I have prevailed in managing several companies to successful outcomes, it certainly isn't my favorite thing to do.

Psychologists and psychiatrists will tell you that most insecurities begin in childhood. For whatever reason, individuals are impacted by some event that makes them particularly sensitive to criticism and judgment. It may be something that was said by a parent, teacher, or classmate. Maybe it's something that was said or done to you that seeks to make you feel different or apart, such as what happened to me as a child in a Native American community. Whatever it is, we all endured episodes that call into question our abilities. We are embarrassed by it, sometimes even humiliated. And we react in a way to not let it happen again.

For me, as I mentioned earlier, it was my stepfather telling me at age fourteen that I was fearful. Even though some elements of what he said were true, that word made me bristle every time he said it. My response: "I'll show you who's scared." What did I do? I took on all the things that would make me brave, starting with becoming a Boy Scout, playing football and basketball, going to medical school, and becoming a pilot and astronaut. I did all these things, in many ways, to prove my strength and courage—to others as well as myself.

In my thirty-plus years of business experience, I've repeatedly witnessed insecurities in others. Two examples stand out: I once had an employee who was challenging, to say the least. They were very smart people, creative, intelligent, and energetic but lacked even the most basic communication skills—not because they couldn't communicate, but because they didn't think they had to. "People should be reaching out to me," they would declare. "Why should I have to reach out to them? They need me more than I need them."

On top of everything, this person was rather immature and had no sense of being a team player. It came to a head during a performance evaluation in which my feedback was extremely glowing, except for their ability to communicate. They immediately got mad and began to cry. They just couldn't take being criticized.

I had never experienced this with anyone. Still, I thought to myself, I can help salvage this employee. So, the next day after they calmed down, I approached them with a supportive manner. What can we do to help you? I asked. It worked for a while, until a few months later when their ego and hunger to be in the right came to the forefront again. This time it was at a critical moment, and their behavior severely impacted an important project. The job required a levelheaded leader to not only manage technical aspects but also the people. Because they lacked this, we lost the opportunity for the company, and millions of dollars.

It was a great disappointment to me personally because I thought they could have been a great leader. But to be a leader, one must be willing to embrace and follow feedback and to acknowledge that we all have drawbacks and challenges. To find and flourish in your place in the world, you must acknowledge your insecurities. Eventually, I had to let them go, hoping they had learned a lesson and would find a better path for the future.

My other experience was with a manager of different character—multi-talented, ambitious, and a hard worker. They were very manipulative and, like the first example, hardly what you would call a people person. They were an enforcer, a take-no-prisoners kind of manager. They guarded their role jealously. They left no doubt who was in charge. Anyone who threatened this was out, one way or another. Unfortunately, I was frequently away from the office, which over time only boosted and emboldened their claim to authority. To be candid, we lost a lot of talented people over the years due to this manager's behavior and attitude.

We all have insecurities that guide how we see and react to the world. The challenge is to recognize them and develop strategies to deal with them in a productive manner that allows us to grow. Once again, that depends on our ability to understand our place in the world, working to become the most we can be while recognizing who we are, warts and all.

FIRST STEPS

This book intends to serve as a roadmap to discover the power within each of us. As I mentioned earlier, I recently re-read

The Secret by Rhonda Byrne, where I learned that the power I found to achieve what I have in life was the same force that she and her colleagues wrote about. Indeed, this power is not a secret but a law that enables all who desire to take advantage of the one force that binds us all.

Subsequent chapters of this book will go into detail about other strategies you can use to find the power in you that leads to understanding your true place in the world. To begin with, here are a few quick ideas you can employ to begin your journey.

1. **Put your mind in reverse.** Find a quiet place to be alone; relax and clear your mind of the activities of the day. Think about your childhood. Go back to when you had no limitations, when there were no obstacles, when the word "no" had no meaning—a time when your imagination was unlimited. Return to that period of unlimited potential. Who were you when there was seemingly nothing to hold you back?

2. **Consider your abilities and talents.** Do an inventory of your talents and skills. I believe we are born with certain skills and abilities that are uniquely ours. So, what are the natural talents or abilities you've always had? From there, add the skills and talents you developed or acquired as you grew older—for instance, sports skills or academic abilities. Take the time to reflect on your natural abilities and learned talents. Knowing these will help direct you to your heart's desires.

3. **What excites you?** Self-discovery requires courage. One of the most unnerving aspects of that journey is being willing to step out on your own, to pursue what matters most to you and makes you happy. That's an essential part of knowing your true self and realizing your full potential.

A close friend once said, "People are going to do the things that are in their best interest." Every time, I would add. People will also think and act to gain an advantage, to avoid someone or something they perceive as a threat, or to soothe pain, be it real or imaginary. This applies whether on the job or in their personal lives. Happily, sometimes it's simply doing what's best for those around us—our children, partner, or family member.

It is not a question of being self-serving or mercenary. It's natural. We are the center of our universe. We embrace the things that make our world better and avoid those that trouble us. We all do it. It's valuable to recognize that in yourself as well as others.

I have a friend who grew up in a well-to-do African-American family. They went to the best schools and seemed to have the perfect life. After completing college, they set out on a career in politics, then academia and later joined a non-profit. Still, even though they did all the right things, they never quite found their groove.

After getting to know them better, I found out that their dream was to get into business. They wanted to get involved with start-ups and become entrepreneurs. We had worked together for a while until they finally got up the nerve to tell me they were leaving to pursue what they truly wanted. Even though I hated to see them leave, I was very happy for them and wished them the best. As I told them, "I am a believer in dreams."

Stepping out on your own can be scary, but it's necessary if you are going to reach your full potential. It's like stepping into a void, as I did during my spacewalk.

That first step really gets your attention. It's terrifying, but it may be where you find your greatest reward.

What areas are naturally appealing to you? What makes your heart skip a beat? Create a list of those things that you want, or wanted, to do, then integrate it with your abilities—the skills that are unique to your being, those things that you do especially well or those qualities for which you are best known. If you don't readily see them, ask your friends. Sometimes, our talents may be invisible to us, but others see them vividly. So, ask.

4. **How do you want to be remembered?** Imagine yourself at a retirement dinner or testimonial. A speaker is going to talk about the successes and highlights of your life. What would you want to hear? Would it be purely professional or touch on other areas of your life? Take a few minutes to make out a wish list. That can be a significant step toward finding your true self and your place in the universe.

These and other strategies that will be discussed at a later point are aimed at fueling the wonderful journey of self-discovery you're about to begin. If we are students of the universe, it is clear to me that each of us must find the power within to find our own way and in our own time. Open your mind to the infinite possibilities of life and find your own path.

I will paraphrase Ralph Waldo Emerson, who wrote, "Once you make a decision, the universe conspires to make it happen."[5]

I truly believe this. It has worked at every step of my life and career: my acceptance into medical school

---

[5]   "Once you make a decision, the universe conspires to make it happen." (Emerson).

at Texas Tech; my selection for residency at the Mayo Clinic; my fellowship with the National Research Council at NASA's Ames Research Center; my selection as a US astronaut; my career in venture capital and asset management; and my philanthropy. The "universe", and in my view, God, were involved in every aspect of success in my life.

5. **Let go of fear.** Early one morning, I was awakened from a dream by my life partner Valerie abruptly leaving the hotel room that we were staying in Nice, France. I reached over the bed, and she was gone. I immediately got up, checked for her luggage, and headed for the door. As I looked out the door, she was halfway down the hall, and I shouted, "Where are you going?" "I am going to work out," she responded. Relieved, I closed the door and tried to go back to sleep. I lay there with this feeling of loss. I was scared and afraid. Of what? Then it dawned on me. I was afraid of her leaving me. I realized in that moment that this must have been how my father felt, so many years ago, when he came home to an empty house. Things were so bad in my parents' marriage that my mother had to escape in the middle of the night. I always sided with her through the years, but I never thought about how my father felt in that moment until now. It must have been devastating for him.

In that moment, I felt relieved by the realization of where my fear came from. I discovered that I have been carrying the sins of my father for years. It explains my anxiety around people leaving me or me leaving them. So, when I saw Valerie leaving that hotel room, I became afraid that she was not coming back. I was afraid that I was not important, that I was not enough, and that I would be alone. I have been carrying my father's trauma and his hurt.

Many of us are trapped by the past. We are living with the things that happened to us. We are caught up in the feelings and the ghosts that haunt our lives, impeding our growth. We must find a way to get past those moments and reach toward the future, where all hope lies. It reminds me of the words that I heard from one of my fellow Horatio Alger member, Quincy Jones, who once said, "The statute of limitations for past hurts and pains are over. Now it's time to look forward."

According to Wikipedia, a statute of limitations, or prescriptive period, is "a law passed by a legislative body to set the maximum time after an event within which legal proceedings may be initiated." This means that our past hurts, transgressions, problems, fears, and so on, have a time limit on our focus and suffering. The time has passed, so we must let them go. When this happens, we will gain a new perspective and view of the world around us. Our lives take on a new meaning and direction that lead us to true fulfillment.

The lesson I want to impart is to let this painful time go. It is in the past, and it will never return unless we relive it in our mind. This can be the most difficult thing to do for many of us. Some of us relish the hurt because of the meaning it gives us. Subconsciously, we want to keep suffering because that may be all that we have to live for. I can tell you that this is no way to live. This is not a life, particularly if you want to live a healthy and fulfilling life. Let it go…move on. Change your perspective.

CHAPTER 2

CHANGE YOUR PERSPECTIVE

....

*"We cannot change the cards we are
dealt, just how we play the hand."*
—Author unknown

....

I grew up in a family of worriers. But my mother elevated her capacity for worry to a whole new level.

One example was the ritual she practiced without exception when we left the house or went to bed at night. She would always check the doors to make sure they were locked, but not in any offhand way. She wouldn't just turn the lock to make sure it was secure. She would first close it, lock it, and then shake it, just to make certain it was locked. Every single time.

She passed that mindset on to her children. Upon leaving the house or just before turning off the lights at night, she would inevitably ask us if we made certain to shake the door.

"Yes, mother," one of us would sigh.

Don't misunderstand. She wasn't coddling us or doing what they refer to today as helicopter parenting. If it were not for her concern for our well-being, I would not be the person I am today. Still, to a young kid at the time, it seemed like overkill.

Not anymore. Some fifty years later, I find myself locking and shaking the door in precisely the same manner. Every single time. And I didn't recognize I did it until Valerie, asked, "Why do you always shake the door?"

"Thank you, Mother!"

My mother came by it honestly. After visiting other members of our family, I realized that habits like this were passed on from our grandparents and great-grandparents. Back in the day, after they received their freedom and ventured west, there was a fair amount of uncertainty. They had to be cautious and careful about their surroundings. This translated into worry and concern. A family story tells of my uncle, who, as a young man in the 1950s, ventured into a small east Texas town, where he was "caught looking at a white woman." In those days, it was a crime. He was murdered by local men simply because of the color of his skin. As young boys, we all heard the story as a warning to be careful of the world that didn't take kindly to Blacks.

As a result of this and other things they experienced, the family was always on edge. I recently read the book *It Didn't Start with You* by Mark Wolynn. He is a psychologist who studied people who had lifelong behavioral problems. Upon deeper analysis, he concluded that many of their issues did not originate with them, but came from their parents and grandparents. These burdens, fears, and problematic behaviors were passed on from generation to generation.

For us, this translated into always needing to know our whereabouts. Where were we going? If we visited a friend's house, which friend was it? When would we be back? Every detail mattered.

DR. BERNARD A. HARRIS JR.

Of course, now I do the very same thing with my daughter and Valerie's children. We are indeed a family of worriers! And of course, we get the same response from our children as we did our parents—particularly since they are millennials—the group whose thoughts and ideas are 180 degrees from their baby boomer parents. But even this habit has been passed on.

Personally, I have carried this cautiousness with me everywhere I go. It feels like I am always under the microscope, needing to watch what I am doing and what I say. I developed a heightened need to be careful and to be better. This has been both a plus and a drawback in my life, although primarily a positive. I've chosen professions that require that things be checked and double-checked. I have to be concerned about details and their impact on others, especially when I am responsible for someone's life as a physician, a pilot, and even as an astronaut.

The cautiousness is a necessary component to what I do. Think about it—would you want to be partnered with an absent-minded astronaut in space? Would you want a surgeon operating on you who's not paying attention to every detail and making sure that there have been no instruments left inside you?

Not me. So, I make it a habit to check, and then check again. Details matter.

Of course, there's a downside to this behavior. Perpetual concern can lead to excessive, needless worry, especially about things you cannot change. As a person who has always been concerned about how things might turn out and trying to figure out all the details, the more I learn, the more I want to know. That means having more things to worry about. But the bottom line is that it is really about balance. You must be concerned about the details but not overly concerned. This description of "My Family of Worriers" is simply a metaphor for the consequences of fear, which can be helpful but if left unchecked could lead to pathology, anxiety, and the disruption of living.

As I grew older, I realized this was no way to live. I became aware of the impact of excessive worry and began working to change it. Otherwise, the fear could begin to interfere in achievement—fear and uncertainty could cripple one's dreams and ambitions.

I know I am not the only one who struggles with this. It begins with doubt, grows into worry, then festers into self-doubt. Anxiety and outright fear are often not very far behind.

Over the years, I realized I needed to shift my perspective. Since fear, worry, and anxiety can be so consuming, it's often hard to overcome the immediacy of the moment. A disappointing turn of events or experience—everything from being teased about how you look to not landing the dream job—seem at the time to be the only reality. Moreover, many of those disappointments can be completely beyond your control.

I came to understand that I needed a place within myself to accept the reality of the event but not to let it distract me. In other words, I needed to find peace in the middle of the storm where I didn't have to share undue space with worry and anxiety.

That meant a change in perspective. It started with the realization that I cannot completely control or influence anyone but myself. Things go wrong and others can have all sorts of ideas and opinions, but those were beyond my reach. I needed to change how I looked at the world around me.

Naturally, being a person imbued with a need to strategize, then check and recheck, I began to create a plan for protecting my newfound psyche. It started with a few core questions:

- What if I truly had peace?

- What if I had faith in good? In right outcomes? In people? In myself?
- What if I truly believed?
- How could I cast off my fears?

In answering these questions, I came to realize that I needed to let go of my worries and my fears as much as I could—not necessarily to cast them off completely (that's pretty much impossible, not to mention foolish), but to place them in a healthier, less dominant perspective. I needed to recognize what I could impact and what I could not.

Again, it made sense. One of my favorite prayers has always been "The Serenity Prayer" written by the American theologian Reinhold Niebuhr (1892–1971): "God, grant me the serenity to accept the things I cannot change, courage to change the things I can, and wisdom to know the difference."

That critical point—to know the difference—has allowed me to change my perspective of fear.

FEAR VS. FAITH

One difference between myself and Valerie is that she sees the world through the eyes of faith. Sadly, I far too often see it through the lens of fear. There are many examples in our lives where this difference is played out. A prime example is when we meet new people. I see their outer persona, how they look, their clothing, their voice, and the tone of their conversation. Valerie sees that too but wants to learn about them personally and what their background is. Where are they from, who are their family, what do they value in life? She does this because she wants to get to know the person and not what they are projecting. I have a lot to learn from her.

Some time ago, we traveled to an event for a dear friend of ours who was getting a major award from their university. Right before the big announcement, Valerie met a complete stranger in the audience. A "miscellaneous person" as we always joke, meaning someone whom you meet who has no relation to you or anyone who knows you. They were in a deep conversation about something I don't recall. It was time for us to go back to our table, stop mingling, and get ready to watch our friend receive their award. I remember getting upset that she was not moving. She said, "They (our friend) already know that I am here, they know that I love them and care about them…but this person has none of that. Something tells me that I need to be here with them." So, she stayed engaged with them, and I stood in for the both of us at the event.

It turns out that this young person was lost and fearful, searching for answers to life's big questions. They needed someone to guide them. I found out later that they were stuck in their career as a music writer and executive. Simply by being there, she was able to give them what they needed to advance their career. Sometimes all we need is for someone to help us find a different perspective. She provided the faith that they needed in that moment.

But it's not an irrefutable truth. Remember the wise guidance of recognizing what you can control and what you cannot; in this case, this change in perspective is entirely up to you.

With eyes of faith, you see the good in people and the world around you. You have the vision of a child, where you are open to things as they come. You are constantly reaching out, looking for the connections and possibilities in life. You truly believe in the good in the world. You dislike negativity and the word "no." You seek freedom at all costs. You love openly and freely. You trust that things will work out, no matter the circumstances. You are a true believer. You are forgiving.

With fear, you see the world as hostile and demanding. You see it as out to get you, ready to trip you up at any moment. You lay awake at night in fear, thinking about all the bad things that could happen. Wondering when the shoe will drop…on you.

You walk around in constant worry about the outcome of everything. You "plan for the best but prepare for the worst." You never like surprises because they are usually negative. Anything except preparing for the worst outcome you consider a fool's errand. Since you see the world as out to get you, you've got to get "them" first.

What's your perspective? Do you embrace the perspective of faith or one more dominated by fear? Thinking about that honestly can help shift your perspective, one that is more fully aligned with your dreams and overall well-being.

SUPERMAN VS. KRYPTONITE

I can't imagine a single American who isn't familiar with Superman's rather horrific relationship with kryptonite. That's why it makes such a useful story to illustrate the difference between fear that merely exists and the sort of fear that can truly be fatal.

As you probably know, kryptonite was the only thing that could kill the Man of Steel. Knives, bullets, bombs, the impact from leaping over tall buildings in a single bound? Not even worth mentioning. But kryptonite was deadly serious stuff.

Looked at in a certain way, fear and worry that effectively compromise your ability to achieve all that you can might be seen as your kryptonite. Excessive fear and worry can lead to irrational decision-making, needless uncertainty, and can ultimately hinder our ability for growth.

Superman was powerless against kryptonite. Happily, we're not nearly as defenseless.

As I discovered myself, a change in perspective can be invaluable in coming to understand what fear is and what it isn't. In particular, it's important to recognize when fear or anxiety are affecting you and those around you. Are you afraid to ask for a promotion at work? Is it because you truly don't feel you're up to succeeding with new responsibilities? What underlying reasons could possibly lead to that perspective? Just as important, what steps can you take to overcome them and change your perspective?

At this point, I have a confession to make. I am deathly afraid of roller coasters and always have been. That's right—someone who has blasted into space at 17,000 miles an hour goes weak at the knees thinking about sitting on a "coaster" going a fraction of that speed. I remember being a teenager at an amusement park when my date urged me to join her on the roller coaster. No way was I getting on that thing, I told her. I stuck to my word, despite my date's teasing about how chicken I was. I stayed off the monstrosity for the rest of the evening.

Did that fear keep me off roller coasters permanently? Absolutely. Did it stop me from becoming a pilot and an astronaut? Not in the least. I just don't like it when someone else is in control.

That's an ideal example of a particular fear that didn't fester into kryptonite. It didn't because I took the time to find the most effective perspective—one that had everything to do with control issues and nothing to do with being labeled as a chicken.

If you think an astronaut who can't stand roller coasters is surprising, how about an astronaut who's terrified of heights? I know one, a very accomplished mission commander. For them, the most intimidating part of the mission is making their way from the elevator at the top of the gantry across the walkway to the spacecraft. They have to lock their eyes solely on the door of the spacecraft to make it to and through the hatch.

Like me, this experienced, successful explorer didn't let fear keep them from achieving their dreams. They, too, kept their fears from becoming their own kryptonite. They didn't let their fears hinder their ambitions, their dreams, or their life. And neither should you!

GETTING TO KNOW WHO YOU ARE

As an astronaut, I have had the opportunity to travel to many places throughout the world in addition to an occasional stroll in outer space. One thing I love about travel is meeting people of different cultures. Both my missions were international, requiring me to train and live in Germany and Russia for periods of time.

I found these two cultures have several things in common. One core trait is that people have to really get to know you before they will accept you. This requires a great deal of time together working and playing. But it is in play where lessons are truly learned. When working, we all put on a professional persona. We act accordingly. But many cultures believe that our true character comes out when we let our guard down and behave according to our true selves—when we're at play.

I recall a very special event during my stint as the representative for the Astronaut Office for training of joint crews in

Russia. One weekend, we were all invited to what I referred to as a "Russian barbecue." Curious as to whether this would involve pit-smoked brisket, my colleagues and I eagerly accepted.

There was one overriding problem. Rather than the warmth of a summer backyard, the party took place in November a few kilometers north of Moscow. Instead of 85 degrees Fahrenheit (29 degrees Celsius), we were standing around in temperatures just a bit above freezing. All of us were wondering, "Why are we doing this?" while trying not to freeze to death.

But of course, there was a remedy for this: alcohol, lots of it. It worked, playing right into the hands of our hosts. Within a few hours of "play" time, we could all see into each other's soul. The event broke the ice—literally and figuratively—and opened the door for more meaningful relationships. It was fun and instructive.

In many cultures, social events are opportunities for people to release their inhibitions. It allows them a glimpse into others' souls and for them to peek at yours. This activity provided just that. We really got to know each other and made tremendous progress training for the upcoming flight now known as the US/Russian Joint mission for Space on STS-63. Most important for me was the realization that if you look beyond the façades that we all have, you will see that we have more in common than not. We are all motivated by similar things such as relationships, family, and dreams.

It also helped me realize that we all inevitably construct façades for ourselves and others. The danger is when we lose sight of who we are in the process. Opening up to those around us not only creates a space of trust and acceptance; it also builds a healthier, more forthright environment, no matter the setting.

Again, it's a matter of shifting your perspective. Not only did we foreigners gain a new perspective from our Russian hosts as to how to get to know others, but it also reinforced the importance of maintaining a perspective of who we truly are, once we squeeze past the persona we often convey to others.

DISCOVER WHO YOU ARE

I have received some of my most valuable lessons about the importance of perspective while running various organizations during my career—both in my interaction with others as well my reaction to them. It makes perfect sense. Most organizations are a microcosm of the world around us with a variety of personalities and motivations. While a few may approach work as just a job to earn money, most of us hopefully join a group because of shared goals.

It also affords us an ideal opportunity to get to know ourselves better.

My journey has taken me through several institutions, from NASA and SpaceHab, to Baylor College of Medicine, University of Texas Medical Branch, Vesalius Ventures, the Harris Institute/ Foundation, and my work at the National Math and Science Initiative. When I reflected on this, I realized that the one common thread that stands out from all others is my desire to make a difference. I have felt that my work has been a journey of self-discovery and fulfillment as well as a sense of truly doing something to make the world a better place. And if that contribution can also help other people enjoy a similarly beneficial and gratifying experience, then the reward is greater.

Since my early childhood, I have always recognized my empathy for people. I have always been concerned about other's feelings and their well-being. I am always looking for ways to help. In high school in San Antonio, Texas, I played the saxophone in the marching band. While at one of our games, I saw someone in the stadium fall ill. There was a rush to assist them. An ambulance arrived but I couldn't get past the feeling of wanting to help in some way. What could I do? I didn't have any medical training. However, I wanted to reach out to them in some way to offer my assistance. That same desire remains with me today. But now I have the medical training to help, which I have done for more than forty years.

This need to help has also led me into both the venture capital business and philanthropy work in education. As a VC, I invest in entrepreneurs by giving them money, time, and insights from my experience. I thoroughly enjoy working with young entrepreneurs, advising and guiding them to a successful outcome. I call them "Young Entrepreneurs" whether they are twenty or sixty years old, because they all are young at heart and excited by their ideas. With regard to education, my philanthropy is all about helping students and their families reach their full potential.

One other story I'd like to share highlights one of my biggest struggles as well as my most important gift. Back when I was twelve, we had moved to another town, Tohatchi, New Mexico, which was part of the Navajo Nation. In a social studies class, we were given an assignment to possibly present to the class. I worked hard on it. I do not remember exactly what the topic of the paper was on, I just know that I was excited by the subject. We all turned the paper in at the beginning of the week for our teacher to read and grade. The following day, after the teacher passed back our papers, I saw I received a very good grade. That was great, but I also remember being deathly afraid that the teacher would call on me. Wouldn't you know it—they did call me up to the front of the class and asked me to read my paper. I was sweating bullets. As I looked at my classmates, I could see them staring at me in expectation of what I would say. I began to read the two-page paper. It went well at first, but I was so nervous that my mouth began to get so dry that I could not even speak. I stopped and asked my teacher if I could go out to the hall to get some water. When I returned, I could hear the other children laughing at me. I was devastated! Despite having done well in the class, when asked to show what I felt was proof my worth, I failed. Even after fifty-five years, that day has left an indelible mark on me.

But this is not the end of the story. Speaking in front of people remains a challenge for me, yet I didn't let it defeat me. In fact, when researchers ask about people's greatest fears, public speaking is always at the top of the list. I am not alone. I decided long ago that I would conquer that demon. So, every time I have been asked to speak, I accept—when I can—as my way of facing my fears. I now look at this as an opportunity to be heard. I remind myself that I have a lot to say because of the blessings in my life. From this, one of my gifts has become communicating with others.

So, that begs a series of important questions. What challenges you? What is your motivation? What drives you to get up for work every day? How can you transform a disappointment or failure into an opportunity?

These are questions that you should be asking yourself. And, if you find yourself in an environment where things are not working—or, for whatever reason, simply isn't as meaningful as it might be—that might call for a change in perspective. Further, it might also call for a change in what you do for a living if a shift in perspective isn't sufficient to provide all that you want and need. Above all, don't be afraid to make a change.

If the root of your dissatisfaction is your job, first, try changing your perspective of the work you're doing now. Consider what it means to you as well as others. How do people benefit from what you do? How are you growing—in whatever context of growth that's meaningful to you—as a result of your work? In short, try to dig a little deeper to understand the why, the significance of your work, from every possible aspect.

I've experienced all types of people with different motivations. I had an employee who declared that they "could be bought." For them, the paycheck was the most important thing in considering a job. Another was solely focused on success or failure. They were driven to succeed at all costs. To be honest, I have a type A personality, driven toward accomplishment. Working with those kinds of people in addition to many others has helped me gain a broader perspective of understanding who I am, including fears, flaws, and all. In other words, dealing with others and their personalities sometimes provides insights into our own.

An employee of mine once did something that, at least to them, was unforgiveable. They inadvertently deleted every file on their computer. Today, since we have spent our entire life on our computers, that's, needless to say, a devastating mistake.

How could they make such an error, especially since I remembered how many times they refused help with the computer issue that ate all their files? The word "stubborn" was also poised on my lips.

But, before all that could leave my mouth, I noticed how disappointed and angry they were with themselves. I immediately switched my mindset to offering how I could help. Although they couldn't locate the files, I was able to find a program that could recover them. With the help of computer experts, they eventually were able to recover the files. Whew! Disaster averted.

But this was not the real issue here. The more important lesson was one that I would later realize—not only how we handle failure but what fears may be fueling that perspective. Although my staffer was hard on themselves in the beginning, they soon realized that what happened was simply a mistake, one that any of us could make at any moment in time. It was a mistake that was not merely correctible but, even had the files been lost for good, far from Earth-shattering.

This shift in perspective was eye-opening for me as an observer because that was certainly not where my head was. I was focused solely on fixing blame and pointing fingers, not unlike my date many years before who laughed at my fear of roller coasters. Instead, once we understood the motivation involved, we quickly moved to that space of peace inside the storm that I referenced earlier. It's essential to note this incident wasn't fixed solely on recovering the computer; my colleague was also focused on recovering themselves. In so doing, others around them had an opportunity to learn about themselves as well.

These and other workplace experiences have shown me how insidious fear and worry can be. As I discovered, anxiety and fear naturally blow consequences destructively out of proportion. And, as my colleague admirably displayed, a shift in perspective can be all that it takes to move away from damaging fears toward a healthier, more balanced perspective.

KERALA–THE VENICE OF INDIA (A SPIRITUAL REAFFIRMATION)

As mentioned earlier in this chapter, I firmly believe experiencing other people and other cultures expands our view of ourselves. It leads us to look at our world differently—a change in perspective—while letting ourselves be seen through another person's eyes. This enhances who we are and what we can be while also focusing our attention outside of ourselves.

Valerie and I were invited to participate in a wonderful trip to Kochi, India a few years ago. After surviving five hours on the road with a very aggressive driver who was hell-bent to get us to the hotel as fast as possible, we arrived. If you have never been on the roads in India, you have missed a wonderful experience of a massive confluence of life, both in the numbers occupying the road, how they're traveling, and with what. The objective is to avoid as many cars, motorcycles, people, and animals as possible while getting to your destination ASAP. When we arrived, the driver smiled with a great sense of pride for their accomplishment. Valerie and I were just relieved we had survived the journey from the airport, let alone the over twenty hours trip from the United States. Whew!

Our host was a group called The Indus Entrepreneurs (TIE), a global organization of entrepreneurs most of whom were of Indian origin. I was a speaker for two of their in-country events in Kochi and Hyderabad. The presentations went off without a hitch, but it was time spent elsewhere that was much more significant.

The hospitality was like no other place we had traveled. The Indian people are a kind and caring group who love sharing their perspective and their world. While in the state of Kerala, where Kochi is located, we were treated to a wonderful trip into the backwaters of Kerala, a beautiful part of the country of endless canals and rice fields in every direction. We explored it via a houseboat, which continuously and slowly traversed the waters for an inspiring trip. Hence Kerala's nickname: "The Venice of India."

We felt as though we had stepped back in history to an earlier place where time itself seemed to stop. We experienced the lives of people going through their normal schedules at a pace much slower than ours, but with no less focus. I was struck by the simplicity. I began to question my perspective on things and on life. Why was I so wrapped up in things that have limited meaning in the big picture? I was reminded how constantly I worried about the little things. In Kerala, however, both Valerie and I could relax and simply be.

In addition to my speaking events, there were several interviews with the local press. I went out of my way to praise the Indian people—one of the most innovative, hardworking, and ingenious group of people I've ever met. We could all learn from them.

But my overall experience also drove me to address more spiritual matters as well. As I noted in the interviews, particularly important to me was the people's spiritual nature and their belief in a high power, in God. Proof positive: The state of Kerala is religiously split—Hindu, Christian, and Muslim. And everyone appears to get along with each other. What an example of tolerance for the entire world.

A few days later, an article came out in a national paper. I used it to convey a message to our family and friends back home.

Family & Friends,

As many of you know, we have been in India for over 10 days now by invitation from The Indus Entrepreneurs (TIE), a group of progressive investors from around the world. Valerie and I have had a wonderful experience networking and learning about the culture of India. The Indian people are warm and very religious. In fact, the country embraces Hindu, Christianity, and Islam, all held together by their common belief in God.

Attached is an article of our visit in The Times of India. Its circulation is the largest in the world. The headline reads "TIME AS AN ASTRONAUT HAS RE-AFFIRMED MY BELIEF IN GOD." Of all the things, I discussed in the interview, they choose my reference to God. This reminds ME to remind YOU that Christmas is a time when we celebrate the life of one who embodied those Godly characteristics many aspire to and the promise of peace for all humankind.

From India, Valerie and I would like to wish you and your families a MERRY CHRISTMAS AND HAPPY NEW YEAR!

This note embodied absolute truth. On both my space flights, I was touched by the sheer beauty that was laid out before us. I remember thinking that this is the image that

God has of our world. I wished that everyone could see it like we astronauts can. Accordingly, I recognize my duty to relay God's message.

CHAPTER 3

FIND YOUR CALLING

....

*"The two most important days in
life are the day you are born and
the day you find out why."*

—Mark Twain

*"Be careful of your words, for your words
become your actions. Be careful of your actions,
for your actions become your habits. Be
careful of your habits, for your habits become
your character. Be careful of your character,
for your character becomes your destiny."*

—Chinese proverb, author unknown

....

BECOMING YOUR DESTINY

As the Chinese proverb cited above states, your words and your actions become your destiny.

This is one of my favorite quotes because it underscores how critically important it is to always be aware of our thoughts and our words. It's so easy for us to get caught up in life, establishing habits early to cope with what life throws at us. But if we are not careful, the reactions that we develop to survive can also become our burden. The words are so simple, yet profound in their impact on our lives.

Every morning for the last few years, I have meditated as part of my overall routine. In fact, the first thing I do after rising from bed is to pray and meditate. It has become easier these days because there are all kinds of apps you can download to train you and help you focus.

For instance, "My Spiritual Advisor," an app which I've found to be very helpful during my daily meditation, often discusses the importance of focus by using the phrase "Right here, right now." We spend most of our waking moments focused on either what happened in the past or what is going to happen in the future. Far too often, we lose sight of the moment.

This reminds me of Yoda in *Star Wars* when he is telling Luke to focus on trying to lift a set of stones while balancing himself upside down. Luke fails, drops the stones, and tumbles to the ground. He complains, "I can't do it, it's too hard."

Yoda responds, "You are never in the present; your mind is always elsewhere and never here." Then he demonstrates the power of the force by lifting Luke's spaceship out of the swamp.

An amazed Luke announces, "I cannot believe it."

Yoda responds, "That is why you failed."

There are many lessons from that movie, which I think I saw when I was about twenty-six years old. It was a highly stressful time as I was beginning my residency at the Mayo Clinic. I was focused on doing well in my training in internal medicine and have set my sights on working for NASA. During my off time, I would read self-help books on how to maximize my personal growth. The timing of the movie's release was perfect, to say the least.

I must admit that focusing on the present has been one of my biggest challenges. All my life has been focused on the future. After all, I am the dreamer. I am the goal setter. I am the planner. My personal work has centered around self-improvement to accomplish my dream: being a physician and an astronaut. When I was twenty-eight, I started running to improve my physical health and performance. Until that point, the furthest I had run was about a mile. I began to systematically improve my skills and stamina to the point of running eight to ten miles at a time. I also lifted weights more, growing stronger, pushing myself to improve my health and wellness.

Additionally, I started working on my research credentials by conducting studies regarding bone loss during long-term space travel. This eventually led to my National Research Council fellowship in endocrinology and later a master's degree in medical sciences. I was focused, determined to ensure that I was more than qualified to meet the criteria to become an astronaut. And when by chance and ordained, I met Dr. Joseph Coombs, a Mayo Clinic physician who worked with the early space program, I felt that I was on course to my mission!

I believe that once your mind is made up—or, said another way, if you truly believe in your heart—the universe conspires to make it happen. I was indeed convinced that it was my destiny. And the rest, as they say, is history.

Ask yourself these life questions:

- What is my purpose in life?
- What are my natural talents, my skills?
- How do I want to contribute to this world?

The answers to these and other similar questions will start you on the road to discovering who you are and charting the course toward your destiny.

DREAM AND IMAGINE

When I was growing up, I loved to watch scary movies. I particularly liked those starring Vincent Price, who could terrify you just by the sound of his voice. Back in the day, he starred in a lot of movies based on books by Edgar Allan Poe. For me, it was a way for me to explore the unknown, push my imagination, and consider other realities.

I believe that considering the unknown and letting your imagination run free encourage dreaming. Apparently, Poe did, too. I found one of his quotes about dreams: "They who dream by day are cognizant of many things which escape those who dream only by night."

Stretching one's imagination is at the heart of developing an inquisitive mind. It's the foundation for seeing yourself in the future. I learned this skill early in life. If you talk to my family and close friends, they might even say that I learned it too well (some occasionally think I'm too inquisitive). In business, we call it "intellectual curiosity." Still, it has served me well through all the things I have done in life thus far.

I believe that to do something you must see yourself doing it first before you do anything else. After seeing Neil Armstrong and Buzz Aldrin walk on the moon when I was thirteen, I was inspired to follow in their footsteps. I remember drawing pictures of spaceships in my notebook in class. Believe it or not, my drawings looked very similar to the vehicle that I eventually flew in (see a copy of my drawing in the appendix). Okay, my drawing may not look exactly like it but, as they say, "It's close enough for government work."

I was certainly a dreamer, especially when I was bored in middle school. The important thing here is that I identified a goal, something that I could reach for and dream about. That's very important for you to achieve anything. Goals must first be imagined, seen clearly in your mind, followed by a belief in yourself and your ability to accomplish those goals. Once you have it set in your mind and heart, you can do anything.

If you can't see yourself doing something at first, at least try to see someone else doing it. That's what I did when I watched the Apollo 11 astronauts on TV. When I decided to become an astronaut, I lived and breathed NASA and the life of an astronaut. I followed the space program, its every mission, crews, and all its successes and failures.

I took one additional step: I imagined myself blasting off into space in my very own rocket ship. In the 1960s and 1970s, there were no Black role models for me to follow. I had to use my imagination, envisioning myself as an astronaut. Living in the middle of the Navajo Nation, far from civilization as it was, I had only the heavens to chart my course. I stretched my imagination in every way possible, fueled by images of astronauts walking on the moon and my dreams to follow in their footsteps. That was my launching pad into the future.

A SHARED ASSET

During meditation one morning, I was thinking about a dear friend of mine who always thought of themselves as a "shared asset." It had always bothered me that they thought so highly of themselves in this way. But for some reason, on that particular morning, I awoke with the realization that they were indeed right. So, I sent them a note to tell them that I finally understood them. I said,

> You are indeed a shared asset. Who you are... your way of thinking and being...the way in which you engage others...your passion for life... your openness...your thoughts...your compassion and your passions...are your SUPERPOWERS and make you an incredibly UNIQUE individual who inspires those around you. YOU ARE A GIFT TO THE WORLD. I LOVE YOU for who you are.

Up until this point, I had always resisted this notion. I thought that they were being arrogant and self-aggrandizing—an excuse to justify their insistent way of always engaging strangers, their need to be with others, and socializing at every opportunity. I later discovered they had developed these skills due to their upbringing, which forced them to rely on themselves and others as a surrogate family. As a result, they developed a set of unique skills that enabled them to become very successful in life and in business.

Sometimes we never realize where our passions and skills come from until some event happens to make us think. Why do I do this? Why am I so emotional about that? Why do I like or dislike the things I do? This type of self-analysis helps you grow as an individual. It's an opportunity to explore how your skillsets have developed and why.

Recently, I met a young Black woman who's a managing partner at very prestigious venture capital firm in Silicon Valley. A very rare person indeed. I asked her why she decided to go into the VC business. Her response surprised me. It was not her choice, she said. She started out wanting to be a teacher. So, she went to a historically black college for her undergraduate degree and began her teaching career.

Somewhere in the midst of teaching, she realized that she wanted to do something different. Not knowing exactly what she wanted to do, she decided to get an MBA. She applied to Stanford University. By chance, there was a class being led by one of the founders of Google, and it was her first exposure to the venture industry. Google is one of the most successful venture-backed companies in the world. She was fascinated by them and in the idea of investing in new companies and their entrepreneurs.

It didn't take long for the founder to realize she was special. He suggested that she might consider getting into venture capital. She initially doubted herself, but with his encouragement, she was able to see the opportunity and, more importantly, her worth. All it took was for someone outside herself to enable the innate talents that she already possessed.

SEEING YOUR WORTH

From the moment we enter this world, we are given boundaries. We are told "no" to teach us how to protect ourselves. Experts have estimated that the average toddler hears the word "no" an astounding 400 times every day (just add that up over a few years and the statistic becomes even more breathtaking).

Understandably, most of these are to protect us. Parents must set boundaries for their children to shield them from the known and unknown. It's essential for the survival of the species.

As an aside, I'm sure that you have heard of the "Darwin Awards." This is the "recognition" given to people who do something so utterly stupid that it results in their death. There are many awards given each year, underscoring the importance of knowing one's limits.

It makes me wonder how many times the woman who worked in venture capital may have heard the word "no" growing up. It may have made them feel they were being held back, limiting them with lower expectations of what their potential was. But all it took was encouragement from another human being to express their thoughts about their potential.

This type of support is incredibly important in a young person's life. For this young woman, it changed the course of her life's journey. To work in venture capital was unheard of in the Black community in which she was raised. Words can be powerful, and actions even more so.

This young Black woman is in the position to become a force in this nation. She also has an incredible heart for giving back, so she is now giving other young people the same gift she has received.

Sometimes it takes someone else to open our minds to the true reality of our nature and enable us to see our worth.

As I've pointed out, background and life experiences, particularly childhood events, are of enormous importance. Through the lens of my own experience of working with youth educational programs for more than thirty years, I firmly believe that we can change the trajectory of our children in four simple ways: EEOC—Exposure. Experience. Opportunity. Culture.

> **Exposure**—One of the most important elements in a child's growth is exposure to positive environments, where they can be nurtured and obtain a sense of belonging.

This is critical during the formative years. They learn right from wrong and good from bad. They begin to learn about boundaries between themselves and the outside world, exploring the limits and their power as individuals.

Experience—The expression "experience can be a hard teacher" describes the foundation of its impact on individual learning. Experience is how we learn most effectively. The more experiences you have, the more knowledge you gain and the more prepared you are for the world. It is the foundation for intellectual capacity.

Opportunity—In order to grow, one must be given opportunities to acquire knowledge (education), to work and explore the world around them. It is the thing that many individuals and communities lack in this country. Without opportunity, hope is limited.

Culture—This is what we are all born into. We have no choice. We simply arrive in the world as part of a certain group and place without any say in the matter. Growing up poor or rich, Black or White, male or female, sets our bias that either has a positive or negative impact on who we are.

Being aware of the impact of these factors can influence and set the direction of our lives. Simply being conscious of them can be the first step toward achieving a high-quality life.

My foundation at one point supported one of the largest summer STEM camps in the country. For more than eleven years, we have partnered with the ExxonMobil Foundation in bringing support and hope to economically disadvantaged youth. Thus far, more than 10,000 students have been served through the program.

The ExxonMobil Bernard Harris Summer Science Camp was a two-week residential program where students are taught using project-based learning and twenty-first century instruction to engage them. For those who may not be familiar with this term, twenty-first century skills are tools that can be universally applied to enhance ways of thinking, learning, working, and living in the world. These skills include critical thinking/reasoning, creativity/creative thinking, problem solving, metacognition, collaboration, communication, and global citizenship.

A key aspect of the program was our Rockstars of STEM. These were scientists, engineers, mathematicians, and others who came to the camp to inspire the students and serve as role models. They were usually young employees within the company who came to speak to the students about their lives, both personal and professional. I have always been impressed by their commitment as well as their individual stories. Many discuss overcoming adversity.

I've met many youths who are trying to find their way. I saw this especially in another of our programs, Dare to Dream, which was geared specifically for elementary students in need of direction. Lacking that direction, perhaps, some would be headed for the juvenile detention center.

The program involves selecting troubled students and matching them with another student who is doing well in school. The idea is to make them part of a unique club whose focus is on making the right choices and improving academic performance. It has been very successful because it provides discipline and purpose.

We offered this program for several years in partnership with Communities in Schools (CIS) in Houston, Texas. Many years after the program began, I was invited to the CIS annual gala. Unbeknownst to me, they had invited a student who had taken part in the Dare to Dream program to introduce me for an award I was to receive. As they stood behind the podium, poised and elegant in their words, they began to tell the story of their difficult background in inner-city Houston, and how the Dare to Dream program saved their life and gave them purpose. Right before they asked me to come up, they announced that they would be heading to Harvard University that fall.

We first met when they were ten years old. This young person had a troubled past. Their mother wasn't in their life. So, they struggled with identity. They turned to destructive behavior. One of the teachers recommended them for the program. It was the first time that someone had taken an interest in them. The program encourages the kids to raise their expectation of themselves. It reminds them of their potential and fosters a belief in themselves through a program of structured lessons. This worked for this particular young person. They discovered themselves and, in doing so, found their dream.

I was so moved by their story—and, more importantly, by their triumph over adversity—that I cried as I walked up the stage. The source of my tears wasn't the award itself but to receive the best reward that a person can have—to know that you have affected another person's life in such a positive way.

It is important for young people to surround themselves with those who believe in them, particularly when they may not believe in themselves. It can make a world of difference in their lives. The motto of the Dare to Dream program is the prescription for success: "To achieve, I must believe and conceive my Dream." This particular young person embodied this in all ways possible.

There are many stories like this from the years of this program and our summer science camp. While the camps are for underrepresented middle school students who have already decided that they would pursue careers in STEM, both programs work to ensure that students are prepared to pursue their dreams by providing the tools, which I believe is a high-quality education. All our programs followed the EEOC principles— expose students to different things, give them positive experiences, provide them opportunities to grow, and change their mindset by broadening their culture. Programs like ours helped many in finding themselves.

When I recalled their stories, I had to include them in this book about finding your calling. Many people are not as lucky as us (these students and me) to know what you want to do at an early age. Some struggle to find themselves and what to do professionally with their lives. So, my mission is to stoke ambitions and incite an internal conversation, with the ultimate goal of helping others discover their dreams.

WHY I DO THE THINGS I DO

A writer was interviewing me for a statewide magazine called *Texas Highways*. They asked me why I did the things that I did. What was my motivation?

To answer that question, I have to return to my story that I told in my first book *Dream Walker*. I started life in inner-city Houston in a neighborhood called the West Side. Back in the day it was a poor area of town, nothing like it is today. The shotgun houses are now being replaced with half-million-dollar homes as rejuvenation takes place and people are moving back into the city.

But back then, we struggled. My loving parents were doing their best to take care of the three of us—my brother, my sister, and me. We didn't know that we were poor or how hard it was for them. There was the added pressure of a struggling marriage due to my father's alcoholism. It was tough all around.

My fondest memories were of Christmas. There was always something under the tree for each of us. I look back now and think about how hard it must have been to make the three of us happy, given those conditions.

As a result, one of my motivations is my desire to ensure that kids and families like mine have a fighting chance in this world. The best way to do this is make sure that individuals have the skills to take care of themselves and their family. I further believe that having quality education is the answer to many of the issues plaguing the Black and Brown communities in this country.

So, my mission is to ensure that we all have the tools we need to fulfill our dreams, no matter what those dreams are. As I wrote in my first book"Dream Walker": firmly believe that all the things that we will ever be already exist within us. All the skills, talents and intelligence are here, in us, at this very moment. We simply need to look for them or in some cases rediscover them."

And as William Raspberry, a Pulitzer Prize-awardee journalist, says, "You cannot accomplish anything in life that is beyond your ability to imagine." It is my job to ensure that people realize these truths as part of their self-discovery. This requires that we are willing to be active participants in our own lives.

As I said in *Dream Walker,* "The greatest loss of all is that many of us never fulfill our dreams, our ambitions, our hopes. This may be a result of our environment, our backgrounds, our fears, or the fact that we simply give up. In my opinion, this is a loss not only for the individual but for all of us, because our world can never benefit from all of those unfulfilled dreams." Said another way, if you do not realize your full potential and fail to accomplish the thing or things that you are meant to do, then it is a loss to the world.

Your task begins with the realization of your worth. Being careful of your thoughts, words, actions, habits, and character ultimately allows you to control your destiny, as the Chinese proverb says.

It starts with your thoughts, how you think of the world. Are you a glass half-full or half-empty person? Do you see the world through "rose-colored glasses" or are you a "Just the facts, ma'am" kind of person?

Your words are usually associated with your thoughts. What you think enters the world through your words and your actions. The things you do every day are an indication of your potential. If done over a long enough period, they become habits, which informs your character and ultimately your destiny.

Many times, when starting out in life, we have no idea what our destiny will be. Some stumble through life, going from one thing to the next until something clicks. Others know from the very beginning what it is they are meant to do. Others wander for a lifetime, aimlessly searching for that thing and never finding it. There are all certainly all sorts of ways to live, but some are not as productive or fulfilling.

My hope is to provide guidance to set you on the path to self-discovery and your destiny. When you realize your place in the world, you become a movement for making a difference and the foundation for the next generation.

CHAPTER 4

BELIEVE IN YOURSELF WHEN OTHERS DON'T

....

*"No one can make you feel inferior
without your consent."*

—ELEANOR ROOSEVELT

*"People may doubt what you say but
they will believe what you do."*

—LEWIS CASS

....

FINDING ONESELF

I believe that the biggest, most difficult task that a person has
to do in life is finding themselves. By that, I mean coming
to understand who you truly are and your true priorities and
goals in life.

But, however challenging, if you don't complete this task,
you will never know what you are meant to do in this world.
I remember as a teenager watching the adults around me and
thinking: "Are they doing what they were meant to do? Is this

the life that they chose for themselves?" Or were they just drifting through life, being pushed by the forces around them, like a leaf in the wind? Wherever they landed, would they just stay and make the best out of it? This was a time where I was trying to find myself, figure things out for my own life. After all, in a few short years I would need to make decisions for my future.

These questions were relevant for my father, who was also lacking direction, never really finding his way. I don't talk a lot about him, because he has been a very sore subject for me for a long time. Remember, my parents divorced when I was only six. They struggled in their marriage from the very beginning.

My father was born in Philadelphia and grew up off Oxford Street (North Philly) in the heart of the Black neighborhood. He was raised with one brother and two sisters. His mother was a strong woman who cared for the children by herself. My father was the baby of the group who particularly adored his brother, the oldest of the four children. My father attended Northeast High School but dropped out after eleventh grade.

Within a few short years, my father found himself in the service working as a military policeman. It is ironic that he would follow in his father's footsteps. He soon met my mother in Temple, Texas, where my grandmother lived not too far from Fort Hood Army Base, where my father was stationed. Fort Hood was officially redesignated to Fort Cavazos on May 9, 2023, in honor of General Richard Edward Cavazos. At the time, Temple was the center of the universe for Black entertainment because of its proximity to the largest Army base in the country. Acts like Ike & Tina Turner, Wilson Pickett, Millie Jackson, and others would frequent the place with its many "joints" in the area. "Joints" refers to a club or bar, and Temple had its fair share of them. The most famous was a place called Meshack's. My understanding is that my parents met at one of these establishments, introduced by my grandmother.

After a short dating period, they married. My father decided to leave the service and get a job in the "real world." It was probably his first mistake, leaving a good-paying, secure career. His other was his addiction to alcohol. It was a lethal combination for a marriage. By the time I turned six, the writing was on the wall. Their marriage would not survive. It was a very painful time for us. The promise of the whole family was lost in the middle of the night as my mother sought a better life for her and her children. What a brave and scary move it had to be for her.

That night was very painful for me, as it marked the separation from my father and the destruction of our family. I still remember it like it was yesterday. During the day, while my father was at work, my mother packed up all our clothes. Even to this day, I really do not know what prompted her abrupt departure—all I know is that she had to leave that day. And so, we did. She loaded us in the cab and we headed for the Greyhound bus station. As we got on the bus, I remember being next to the window, the glass cold to the touch. Finally, the bus took off on our way to my grandmother's house in Temple.

I remember resting my head against that window and looking out at the passing scenery, with the backdrop of a full moon. We had escaped! Escaped from what? A life fraught with uncertainty and potential disappointment? I didn't know, and perhaps neither did my mother.

For me, it was my first test of resilience. It was a call for inner strength and a contemplation of my future. Of course, I did not use these words, nor did I have these introspective thoughts at the time. What I did feel was the pain of loss and uncertainty. What was going to happen to us? Why did this have to happen? Where are we going? What does our future hold? To put it succinctly, I was scared. As I write these words, those feelings are still with me. The pain and anguish of that period in my life are still fresh. I cannot imagine what my mother must have been feeling, too. After all, she had three children to take care of in addition to herself. But her decision would change the course of our lives for the better.

It is in moments like these that we can sometimes find ourselves: moments of uncertainty, pain, and stress. They force us to go deeper than we would have otherwise, as it did for me. This moment made me more introspective and contemplative, beginning the process of looking to the future as a distraction from the present. Surely the promise of the future must be better...better than now. So, I became a dreamer. I developed the skillsets that became the core of my success.

SUCCESS IS A CHOICE

As I write this, I am well aware of my point of view as a believer who always wants people to choose to do their best. The important word is "choose." We all have decisions to make in life, whether we want to be successful or choose—perhaps inadvertently—not to succeed. I remember telling a young friend, who struggled early in life as do many young people: "It is your choice whether to accept success or failure." I believe that the outcome is dependent on when we first decide to achieve and how we deal with the failures that will eventually come our way. I believe success is a choice, that we make. But failure can also be a choice.

I had a classmate whose child struggled to find their way. They did well in high school and, in fact, was inducted into the

National Honor Society. When they applied to college, they got into all the colleges and universities on their list. I remember their parents being so overjoyed at this accomplishment. So, they went to their first choice.

Things went well for the first semester; they joined the right clubs and took part in extracurricular activities. But then something happened. Gradually, they became distant, not calling their parents on a regular basis. They began to withdraw from college activities. When their parents finally talked with their child, they realized that they were severely depressed. Why? What happened? After multiple discussions and counseling, it was discovered that they had a hard time adjusting to campus life. More importantly, they found dealing with the personalities of some students extremely difficult. They were not prepared for the social aspects of college life. In retrospect, they were academically prepared but not worldly prepared. Severely depressed, they had to drop out of school.

It turns out that this happens to many people, particularly young people who are ill-prepared for the world. Many times, this is the first significant failure in a person's life. I believe many of us are simply not prepared because we do not understand ourselves and our motivation.

I firmly believe that if they had, it could have been a different outcome for them. But I also believe that it is never too late to learn from the trials in life. Some of our greatest lessons come from life experiences, but they can also be our toughest.

LIFE QUESTIONS

How can you avoid that sort of discouraging story? Another version of the exercise that I mentioned before involves answering the "life questions."

Life questions are the things you ask yourself when no one else is around. The reason for this is because you want your focus to be exclusively on the questions and have the solitude and comfort to be completely honest.

- Who am I?
- What do I really, really want?
- What is truly meaningful? What is my purpose?
- How do I give back?

These questions are for the soul. They encourage you to look deep within yourself to find who you are. In doing so, you will discover your true calling. I am convinced that when you find your true calling, you will be happier and more successful than you can ever imagine.

Several years ago, my daughter decided to prioritize her personal growth. She took some time off from everything—from her friends, colleagues, her family...even me. Needless to say, I was not happy. I couldn't understand why she wasn't returning my phone calls. Why, when we did talk, the conversations were short and superficial.

Finally, I asked her. "Why are you treating me this way? Did I do something wrong? It seems as though you are mad at me for some reason."

After a few tries, she confided in me that she was working through some personal matters . She said to me: "It's not about you, Dad."

Whoa! What do you mean?

She was trying to convey that she needed time and space to process. More importantly, she needed to do it without me. Granted, as parents we expect this at a certain point in a child's life. I needed to let go and give her the space to think and spend the necessary time to process things for herself. In that moment, I found it hard to let go. I was used to her including me in moments like this. Until that point, we would become closer during the tough times, not more distant. We relied on each other, so it hurt because I felt shut out. Any parent of a teenager could certainly relate. And perhaps, my own mother felt this way with me. After years of reflection, I now understand that she needed me to let go so she could continue to grow.

It was one of the more difficult things that I have ever had to do. To let go of my baby girl was not easy. We all have been through this at some point in our lives when we need space and time to be introspective, to discover who we are without anyone else's expectations or inputs. These can be defining moments that can change the course of our lives. As a result of this, my daughter has become a powerful person who has accomplished a great deal. She is self-reliant, strong, and resilient.

I learned in the process that sometimes we must let go of those we care about so they can learn to care for themselves. Our will and expectations for them are simply that…our expectations, not theirs. Letting go can be the most powerful gift of all. One of my favorite quotes is by Emmet Fox: "Your heart's desire is the voice of God, and that voice must be obeyed sooner or later."

So, the earlier we choose to take the time to discover ourselves, the sooner and more complete our lives will be. It was the hardest thing that I have ever done…the hardest thing I continue to do. The process never stops if we are to continually evolve. Finding out who we are is a difficult task; it requires us to spend time alone with our thoughts. It is a discovery that involves learning who we are.

Here is an exercise I would like you to try. Find a quiet place where you will not be disturbed. Ask yourself the following questions. Think about them and then write down the answers.

WHAT

- What do I like?
- What really excites me?
- What do I enjoy?
- What is my favorite activity? Music, sports, exercise, movies, reading, and so on?
- What is my favorite sport?
- What is my favorite instrument?

WHY

- Why do I like it…?

HOW

- How does it make me feel?
- How do I feel when I…?

WHO

- Is there someone doing something similar?

Find someone who is doing what you would like to do, a mentor or a role model. Then just ask them: WHO are they? WHAT are they doing? WHY are they doing it? HOW did they do it?Finally, ask yourself if you can do the same thing or something similar. Try it. Test it. How does the image of what you decided to do make you feel?

I use a very simple barometer for deciding if something is a fit. I ask myself if this is a head and heart decision? Meaning if what I chose with my head, and it also feels good in my heart, it most likely the right decision for me.

As a child, I did this in my own way. I didn't do it exactly in the fashion that I just outlined. I have already synthesized the basic parts for clarity and better understanding, and made the tasks actionable. Nevertheless, because of this work I was better prepared for the world. Plus, I had one big advantage over my peers. I had a goal.

If you choose, you can, too. This is an act of will despite what is happening to you now. You can be the captain of your ship, the master of your soul. But it takes work on your part. Many have taken the easy way out by giving in to the urges of the world, taking shortcuts by letting others direct their paths.

Let me explain. When we let go of the reins of our life, this leaves room for others to influence us, often in negative ways. When you are directionless, listening to others can draw you into things that are not good for you, like a child joining a gang in the inner city to fit in. Your whole being can become trapped by the short-term reward of being part of something greater than yourself. In this case, you can potentially lose yourself in the process. This happens because you do not truly understand your full potential.

I have a dear friend whom I have respected for many years. She was a woman of means before she married one of the most powerful men in the country. She quit college to be with her husband prior to him heading off to the Korean War. Her husband managed to survive the war and they eventually had three beautiful children, leading a storybook life together until her husband's passing. Shortly afterward, she changed. She was no longer the loving person that I knew, the person who seemed open to people's differences, to being less tolerant of others' life choices, more critical and judgmental.

She forwarded me the following quote by Thomas Sowell in response to George Floyd and the movement against systemic racism: "No society ever thrived because it had a large and growing class of parasites living off those that produced."

I believe she got caught up in the dogma of the far right and the convenience of self-righteousness. For weeks, I tried to wrap my head around this change in her personality. Was it caused by her husband's death or was it there all along? I really don't know. As you can imagine, we have not talked in a while.

My guess would be that upon her husband's death, she found her voice. I may not like what she is now saying but at least she is free to believe and say what she wants. Is this her new voice? I will never know.

This is what finding your voice means: discovering the freedom to be who you are, even at the expense of shocking and possibly alienating others; to release the bonds of social norms and expectations of others and utilize this freedom to explore who you are and what you want to be. Knowing who you are allows you to be open to those paths that are synergistic to your being, allowing for greater fulfillment. The lesson is; don't let others define you or fall victim to the outside world.

Janet Jackson says it best in a post on Instagram based on a quote by Dave Willis:

Just Keep Swimming

Sometimes those around you will not understand your journey. That's OK. It's not their path. It's yours. Remember, "if you live for people's acceptance, you will die from their rejection".

So don't worry about other people's opinions of you. God never told you to impress people, only to love them. Also, try to then make a conscious effort to surround yourself with positive, nourishing and uplifting people. People who believe in you, encourage you to go after your dreams, and applaud your victories.

Above all, stay strong.

FINDING STRENGTH THROUGH FAITH

My life has been filled with examples of how faith has intervened. Faith allows you to believe in yourself when the world turns its back on you. My faith started with my family. My great-grandmother was the originator of our family's faith in ourselves and each other. This is a woman who had five children and who was widowed early in life. I believe it was her faith in God that sustained her. That faith has been passed on to the next generations.

In preparation and training for my first mission, we had several setbacks that tested my faith. I lost count of the number of delays because of mechanical issues with our space shuttle, which culminated in the outright failure of one of our engines right before launch. After that disappointing day, I recall returning to the astronaut beach house, which was used for celebrating the pending launches with family and friends. But this time, I was there alone, walking the beach wondering if I would ever get a chance to leave this planet. As I write this, it seems so funny to be saying these words…"leaving the planet." My faith was pretty low. And as I do when I am in this state, I turned to the Bible and found this passage,

> You whom I have taken from the ends of the Earth, And called from its remotest parts, And said to you, You are My servant, I have chosen you and not rejected you. Do not fear, for I am with you; Do not anxiously look about you, for I am your God. I will strengthen you, surely I will help you. Surely I will uphold you with my righteous right hand. —Isaiah 9:9–10, King James's version

The words were not only comforting for me, but they also spoke to our predicament. Here we were trying to fly into space where we could have God's eye view, and Isaiah seems to have captured our frustration and desire. Suddenly, I was truly comforted and believed that this thing that I had wanted to do all my life would happen. We stood down for about a month until the engines were replaced, and all systems were ready. On April 26, 1993, Space Shuttle Columbia and its crew launched into space for a ten day mission of science.

My faith was tested, and it wouldn't be the last time.

THE ROLE OF FAITH

What is the role of faith? For me, it is a necessary element for success and achievement in life. Without it, it is easy to succumb to the trials and tribulations of life. Faith gives you the strength to face disappointments and carry on when your circumstances say otherwise. Sometimes, when faced with adversity, it can be easier to fold, to pack up and go home. To give up.

It is faith that assures you that everything will be all right. Sometimes it is as simple as taking the next step toward your goal…then the next, until you eventually find your destination.

The basic challenge of my early life was that I was not seen by those in power to be worthy or even having the ability or capability to be. Growing up, my childhood was marred by loss, stereotypes, and outright opposition. But my faith in God and in myself wouldn't allow me to buy into that narrative.

THE IMPORTANCE OF FAITH

Why is faith important? Faith is the one thing that no one can take from you unless you give them permission. It is an action that enables inner strength. It, by definition, requires active participation on your part. I have said earlier that success is a choice, a choice that you make. Well, so is faith. This is why it is so important. Nothing great can be accomplished without it. Faith helps you cast away your doubts. When others doubt you or try to hold you back, or you begin to doubt yourself, remember that you are a child of this great universe with an important role to play. You are more than you realize; you are an important part of this world. Start by having faith in these words.

BELIEVE IN YOURSELF

Believing in yourself is one of the most important things you can do for yourself and those around you. If you don't believe in yourself, how do you expect others to believe in you? If you do not have this perspective, you are doomed to a limited existence.

I am a child of the 1960s and 1970s, where I was constantly reminded of my place and role in American society. Seeing the daily examples of racism was a constant reminder of lack and limitation, particularly at the highest levels. To this day I recall the systemic, unspoken racism of applying to and being accepted into medical school. Since I was Black, there was an undertone that I did not belong. The same held true for women and people of varied races and religions. Even if you excelled, it was treated as an aberration, a freak occurrence. That, or you were one of the "good ones"—the exception to the rule that nobody dared mention.

It took me a while to realize that despite my accomplishments, I have always struggled against the forces that seek to hold me down. Why is it this way? It is a combination of nature and nurture, as with many things. A large part of it came from being Black in this country and world—where we are treated differently than Whites. Many have a history of privilege, while ours has a history of slavery.

Systemic, cultural, and embedded attitudes, views, bias, actions, and policies not only cement preference for one group, but also purposefully hold another group down. This whole notion is not true unless we want it to be. We have a choice as human beings to think differently and to be different.

That's why it's imperative to believe in yourself. It is the reason that I am so driven to achieve—to prove to the world and myself that I am just as good, if not better. It is at the heart of not being enough. Because to some of the world, I will never be. In those times when and where I am proven as good or better, there is the constant reminder that I am not—except for what I believe about myself.

How does one break the cycle of this madness? By first recognizing it and being mindful of its influence and impact on one's life. Then, by knowing who you are and what you are capable of, no matter what others or society might say. Other writers before me have pointed out this truth.

Kahlil Gibran says, "When you are born, your work is placed in your heart." Henry David Thoreau states that, "If a man does not keep pace with his companions, perhaps it is because he hears a different drummer. Let him step to the music he hears, however measured or far away." And Wayne Dyer writes: "Nothing can make you happy or successful. These are inner constructs that you bring to your world, rather than what you receive from it."

All these writers and philosophers found the truth through their own path. And in doing so, they were placed on a road of self-discovery that resulted in their elevation of consciousness.

THE SEARCH FOR MEANING

By now, it should be obvious that I have always been fascinated by the search for meaning in life. I've always sought out those who could help me on this journey, people whom I could learn from. I sought those with the wisdom of the ages—mentors from near and far, people whom you may not know but who have inspired you in some way. People whom you have learned from or taught you a lesson or two.

For me, one of the first people who fell into this category were the original astronauts—John Glenn with his first orbit around the planet, followed by Neil Armstrong and Buzz Aldrin on Apollo 11. They were my inspiration to become an astronaut. Dr. Martin Luther King Jr., Malcolm X, and John Lewis were critical role models during a difficult time in American (United States) history. I did not know them personally, but they became important in my growth into who I am today. Additionally, there were people whom I knew personally who were instrumental in my growth: my mother, stepfather, uncle, aunts, and sister. And many others along the way.

That begs the question. Who are your mentors? Do you have anyone who has helped you? Who has your back, especially when things get rough?

I recently heard a story about the power of a mentor. I have a friend who has described their upbringing as poor. They were one of five kids, growing up in rural America in a home with no running water or indoor bathroom. Their mother did everything possible as a single parent to take care of them. They were a smart and inquisitive child, good in school but their opportunities were limited.

In high school, they had to get a job to help the family. They had the good fortune to be hired by someone who took a liking to them. They excelled and felt supported. The owner of the company recognized their potential. When my friend had the opportunity to advance in the company, the owner fired them—so they could go to college. Even more, the owner helped them get their first job and supported them financially and, just as important, emotionally. They owe their career to this man—a career which, as I write this, currently includes the presidency of a major aerospace company.

This story is a testament to the "power of one"—one person who discovered their talents and believed enough in themselves to use them. It is also the power of someone else who believed in them. That's a powerful combination!

When I look at my life, I cannot help but acknowledge that my path to success came from the people that I encountered, not to mention a good dose of blessings. If it were not for my forefathers and foremothers paving the way for my ascension, I would be nothing. I owe a great debt that I can never repay, so I pay it forward by enabling the next generation and the next so that the future occupants of this world and especially my community can be their own affirmative action.

CHAPTER 5

FAILURE—GREAT TEACHER, POOR CHOICE

....

"Success is a lousy teacher. It seduces smart people into thinking they can't lose."
—BILL GATES

"Success is not final, failure is not fatal: it is the courage to continue that counts."
—WINSTON CHURCHILL

"Strive not to be a success, but rather to be of value."
—ALBERT EINSTEIN

....

Gene Kranz had it right—somewhat—when he "said" failure is not an option.

The 1995 film *Apollo 13*, which dramatized one of the most chilling moments in the history of the US space program, featured this iconic line, spoken by Ed Harris playing flight director Kranz. Harris/Kranz was referring to efforts to rescue three astronauts—Jim Lovell, Jack Swigert, and Fred Haise—after their moon-bound spacecraft malfunctioned. The widespread damage not only scratched the landing itself but also led to a desperate scramble to return the three men safely to Earth.

You've probably seen it. It's a powerful movie. But, of course, being from Hollywood, certain liberties exist. Perhaps the most glaring was the actual source of that famous phrase. Kranz never said it. Rather, it was another member of the Apollo 13 mission control crew, FDO Flight Controller Jerry Bostick, played by actor Ray McKinnon (best known for his impassioned plea to allow the spacecraft to use the moon's gravity to slingshot it back toward Earth: "It's the option with the fewest question marks for safety.").

No matter the actual source, the announcement that failure was not a choice has evolved into an often-used motivational remark.

But, as I alluded to earlier, it's not entirely accurate. For one thing, failure is often an outcome forced on those struggling to succeed. In the case of Apollo 13, any number of things could have occurred. Perhaps the rockets could have exploded when they were reignited. Maybe the support team back on Earth couldn't come up with a solution to replace the mismatched air filter cartridges. Those trying to save the astronauts certainly wouldn't have chosen any such events to take place, but they very well could have happened. In this case, failure could have been an "option" imposed on those literally involved in a life-and-death situation.

But, for me, Harris/Kranz's comment carries greater significance. First, for far too many of us, failure is, in fact, an option. When we give up on something, if we concede that we're just not capable of doing something, we're making a choice to freely embrace failure. Sometimes, that makes sense. If we determine as empirically as possible that something simply isn't going to work, it's only reasonable to just move on.

But it's what happens after that that truly matters. If we let failure carry greater weight than it deserves—if, in effect, we let it define us—then failure becomes something much more than it truly is. It becomes a part of us, particularly so if we're the ones choosing to fail by simply giving up. It's a scar we choose to wear.

On the other hand, if we treat failure as an opportunity to learn and grow, then it becomes something much more meaningful than a frustrating setback. It's a chance for us to get better. It reinforces our sense of reality. It can change character in ways we can't imagine. If we are truly honest in our consideration of failure—if we look for what really occurred rather than searching for the answers that we hope to find—we can learn how to transform the experience of failure into resiliency.

On the other side of the coin, for all its cosmetic appeal, success can be a lousy teacher. As Bill Gates noted in the quotation cited at the beginning of this chapter, it can convince even the smartest, most gifted of us that we can do no wrong. We're invincible, immune to mistakes. While self-confidence is undoubtedly a wonderful trait—one that's essential to realizing our full potential—too much can blind us from the reality that we're prone to mistakes every so often.

That's where failure can get a shot in the arm. Any of us who are certain that we're beyond making any sort of mistake can be absolutely devastated when the "unthinkable" happens. We mess up, we make the wrong choice. For someone who's lived in the alternate reality that is infallibility, mistakes can prove to be soul crushing. It can serve as a blank check to blame anyone or anything else for our failure.

That's why success, ironically enough, can be a mixed blessing. It doesn't have to be that way, though, provided we shift our perspective about how we view our successes and failures and come to learn which of the two truly commands our attention.

TO THINE OWN SELF BE TRUE

As I mentioned before, I have always been curious. It has worked to my advantage and has also landed me in a fair share of trouble. The tipping point between those two outcomes has often been a matter of confidence gone too far—that I could do certain things I really wasn't capable of.

My earliest recollection was when I was in elementary school in the West End in Houston. We used to play under the fig tree in our backyard, where we would pretend to be soldiers defending our territory from the enemy. I had a good friend named Donald. Donald and I used to play for hours. Donald was very much like me: we were curious about everything.

One day, inquisitive as always, we decided to explore the element of fire. Accordingly, Donald and I thought that our play area needed a fireplace. So, we hatched a scheme to get money from my father so we could buy matches to start the fire. The plan worked well—my little brother and I asked our father for five cents, claiming it was for candy. Then we hurried to a nearby store to buy the matches, telling the clerk that they were for our dad.

Having effectively executed the mission, we immediately went back to our treehouse in the backyard and began to build a fire. It was a very successful venture—a little too successful, in fact, because within a few minutes, we had a roaring fire that almost consumed the tree. We managed to put the fire out, but not before my father found out what we did. He was not pleased. (Lesson learned: Don't play with fire, because it will burn you in more ways than one.)

Then there was the time that I took my brand-new covered red wagon apart that I had just gotten for Christmas. While playing with the drawstring on the canopy, I accidentally pulled it entirely out of the cover. For the life of me, I could not put it back in. So, I had the bright idea to cut away the fold of the material that held the string. Then it was just a matter of laying it on top of the material of the canopy, folding it over with string in it, and sewing it back together. Simple!

By the way, did I mention that I had never sewed anything in my life? I watched my mother do it many times, so how hard could it be? I was about halfway through when Mother stepped in and put an end to my ingenious project. As my sore behind could attest, I had the vision but not the ability to carry it out.

As you can tell, I had a wild imagination as a kid. I thought there was nothing I couldn't do, even though I often did not have the prerequisite talent or skills to match. On the one hand, I never wanted to lose my curiosity or sense of adventure—and I haven't. On the other hand, I also learned that understanding what I'm capable of and what I'm not is central to any task or challenge that I might take on.

Over time, I began to recognize and appreciate both my skills and weaknesses, which circles back to how we view success and failure. By striving to know myself, I was able to keep success in perspective—if I knew I was good at something, then success made sense. At the same time, by knowing my weaknesses as well, I could treat so-called "failure" as an opportunity to strengthen something at which I was less skilled.

It comes back to Shakespeare's *Hamlet* and Polonius's admonition to his son Laertes: "This above all; to thy own self be true." In other words, take the time to get to know yourself and to first act with your own best interests in mind. Knowing yourself lets you approach success and failure with the healthiest mindset possible—one that allows you to enjoy success without attaching any undue meaning to it and treating failure as an opportunity to learn and grow. If you work to understand what defines you, you'll not only be set up for success, but you'll also be prepared to make the most of those experiences that are something less than successful.

To be clear, the importance of prioritizing yourself isn't self-serving or being indulgent. Rather, it involves understanding the inherent chronology in our relationship with ourselves and others. Simply put, you can't be of service to others before you honestly know yourself and what you're capable of doing. That's why every pre-flight instruction stresses the necessity of putting on your own oxygen mask first before attempting to help anyone else. First and foremost, take care of yourself. That way, you can do the most for those around you.

FAILURE CAN POINT YOU
IN NEW DIRECTIONS

It's evident that failure can be the best teacher any of us can have, provided we approach it with the attitude of learning all that we can from the experience. Sometimes, failure can also change the course of your life—and all for the better.

I initially applied to be a member of the astronaut corps in 1987, near the end of my fellowship in endocrinology at NASA Ames Research Center, in Moffett Field, California. At roughly the same time, I met a neighbor at a party who happened to work at NASA. When I asked if they could suggest anything to strengthen my candidacy, they suggested I travel to Houston (I was in California at the time) where they would introduce me to Joe Atkinson, head of the Equal Opportunity Employment Commission (EEOC) there. They told me Joe was a member of the astronaut selection committee and could prove to be a huge advocate for me.

So, I traveled to Houston and met with Joe who, in turn, introduced me to several other folks at NASA Johnson Space Center. They encouraged me to apply, which I did. I got an interview, and they performed the necessary background check. All signs pointed to my joining the class of '87. As the run up to the announcement of candidate selection approached, I could hardly contain my excitement.

Shortly before the selection announcement, however, I received a phone call from Carolyn Huntoon, who, if I recall correctly, was the assistant director of the Johnson Space Center at the time. The moment I heard the tone of her voice, I knew something wasn't good.

"Bernard, I'm sorry," she said, "but you haven't been accepted into the astronaut corps this year. But we would like to offer you another job."

I later learned that I had, in fact, been part of the group initially selected to be astronauts. As it happened that year, as the list wound through the approval process, they decided to reduce the number of people in the program for that particular year. But the selection committee didn't want to cut the rest of us completely loose, so they offered us jobs to keep tabs on us for the future.

I was naturally disappointed at the time but decided to take the job offer. After completing my fellowship, I went to work as a clinical researcher for Dr. Victor Schneider, head of the bone laboratory at the Johnson Space Center. It turned out to be a life-altering experience. Not only did Dr. Schneider mentor me personally, but he also encouraged me to take my work even further to help in research regarding the impact of space travel on the human body.

After some fits and starts, I was assigned to join a program to design the healthcare system for crews in space. It was a new project in which we helped develop the medical equipment and hardware necessary for both the space shuttle and the space station. Ultimately, I was put in charge of countermeasures—the tools and procedures necessary to counter the effects of space on human beings.

It was a wonderful immersion in the evolving field known as space medicine. At the core of it is space adaptation syndrome, which is the body's ability to adjust to microgravity. Even for a medical professional, the work was eye-opening. I learned that microgravity impacts every physiological system in the human body. It results in the loss of 1 percent of bone mass every month. We lose as much as 15 to 20 percent of our muscle mass. Our hearts become smaller because they don't have to work as hard. Due to changes in our immune system, we cannot fight illnesses as effectively anymore as we would on Earth.

My new job was to take on everything that could occur to the human body in space and devise effective countermeasures. At the heart of these changes was inactivity. In space, there is very little gravity, which we refer to as microgravity. My research involved work developing exercise programs and the necessary medical/exercise equipment to decrease the effects of space.

As it turned out, my rejection from the astronaut program allowed me the opportunity to become a leader in the earliest stages of NASA's life sciences program. I would never have become a "space doctor" if it hadn't been for that earlier disappointment. My so-called "failure" steered me toward an immensely rewarding and important experience.

It also raised my profile within the astronaut program. When the next pool of applicants was considered in 1990, I was one of the first candidates invited for an interview and selected.

"FAIL" AND MOVE ON

I was certainly fortunate to have failed in my first attempt at joining the astronaut corps. But it involved much more than the opportunity to participate and grow in a cutting-edge field of space medicine. It also afforded me the chance to move on quickly from that initial jolt of being rejected.

That's another downside to fixating on success and fearing failure. When we fail—and inevitably we all do—it can be hard to move past it. We blame ourselves and scour our memory for that exact point when something "went wrong" or we "screwed up." We become so immersed in any number of destructive emotions—resentment, disgust, self-criticism—that we forget to put it behind us and prepare ourselves for what very well may be a life-changing blessing—as happened with me. Instead, we wallow in the imperfection of the moment. We choose to trap ourselves.

That's not to say that we shouldn't examine the mistakes we make in life. Absolutely! But learn what you can from the experience, forgive yourself, and move on. If we choose to wallow in a dark place of disgust and resentment, we lose in any number of ways. And, as a medical doctor, I can only caution that such prolonged periods of self-induced stress and anxiety can have tremendous health consequences, from gastrointestinal problems to post-traumatic stress disorder (PTSD).

"FIFTEEN MINUTES OF FAME AND FIFTEEN MINUTES OF SHAME"

There is nothing to be gained by dwelling on failure and all its associated issues and problems. Whatever it takes, let them go.

Here is where I remind you again of one of my favorite sayings: "fifteen minutes of fame and fifteen minutes of shame." Life is full of things that we do that bring us positive outcomes and affirmations but also times where we fail and are disappointed in ourselves. We must keep a balance in life because there are lessons and opportunities in both. Sometimes we can get caught up in the fame, thinking that we are so important, while in other times we wallow in despair and hopelessness because of our losses.

I believe that if we allow only fifteen minutes for both, we neither become overconfident nor depressed. In other words, we find balance. Try spending fifteen minutes celebrating your accomplishments and the same in wallowing in your disappointment. All things in balance. You will become a better person as a result.

CONTROL WHAT YOU CAN

When it comes to the issue of success versus failure, it's valid to recognize that, for some people, the decision can be a bit pre-ordained. I'm referring to a variety of people—people of color, the LGBTQ+ community, women, just to name a few—who believe they are often denied the opportunity to succeed because of who they are, what they look like, or who they love:

> "I didn't get the job because I'm Black."

> "They promoted Bill because they wanted a man in that job."

> "People on the steering committee didn't want me there because they're homophobic."

It would be intellectually dishonest to argue that such attitudes don't exist. They certainly do. We see and hear about incidents involving that sort of bigotry every day. Although some claim that sort of behavior is changing, it's still very much around and many still have to cope with it.

So, if you feel you can be vulnerable to that sort of thinking, how can you best handle it?

To begin to consider that question, I'm reminded of something an acquaintance of mine—a white, gay man—once told me.

"Bernard," he said, "when I walk into a room, I can show up as a white male or I can show up as a gay person. When you walk in, you don't have a choice."

His comment struck me with its insight. As a person whose "differences" are on the inside, as it were, he had the option of coming across to others any way that he wished.

As a Black man, even though I can speak and behave in whatever manner that I like, I can't change the color of my skin. And, if others have a bias regarding that, it may very well have an impact—in a board of directors meeting, during a fundraising pitch, or in an interview for a new job or position. To be honest, it can be tempting to attribute some experiences to that sort of bias. If they turn me down, was it because of my skin color? Were they more concerned about what I look like than what I had to say?

Again, I cannot change who I am, at least so far as my race. But what I can impact is how I come across to others, the color of my skin notwithstanding. I can be as prepared as I possibly can be. I can work to have my credentials as complete and impressive as possible. I can prepare whatever I have to say with the utmost care and attention. In short, I can focus as much as I can on what I can influence and pay less attention to those factors that are up to others to change.

Here's a story that illustrates that. In 1978, I arrived in Lubbock, Texas to attend medical school. There was a welcome/orientation meeting where we were all introduced to each other. You can imagine this young man from inner-city Houston being transplanted to a small West Texas town. The cultural differences were obvious—I was a fish out of water. I recall thinking, "What have I done? Am I going to be able to survive in this environment?" These questions were poignant since I was the only Black in my class. (As I mentioned earlier, there were only two other Black students in the entire medical school.)

So, I had to make up my mind that I was going to stay, despite the challenges before me. I was fortunate to meet my best friend during the orientation meeting, a young man from Midland –Odessa, Texas, a place even further west. After getting to know Michael Robertson and later his wife Lisa, I found out that the only Black people he had met before me were the guys he played football with in high school. For some reason, we were drawn together then and remain close to this day.

I had to put aside my fears and focus on our similarities, not our differences. I needed to affirm my right to be there and demonstrate my intellect and abilities. It was probably the first real test of courage for me.

That approach is inevitably far more effective than merely assuming that who you are dictates outcomes. In fact, that can be something of a crutch. I've known many people who believe they've been held back because of their race, gender, or some other reason. Far too often, that can prove to be nothing more than an excuse for mediocrity—a search for reasons other than the fact that they didn't come across well or lacked necessary experience or credentials.

So, work to control what you genuinely have control over. If someone else treats you differently because of who you are or what you look like, remember that's much more a reflection of them than of you.

EMPHASIZE VALUE, NOT SUCCESS

Recognizing the true nature of success and failure is central to our growth as human beings and to our efforts to become more self-aware. In fact, it can also lead us to the revelation that, in many ways, success and failure aren't really what matter most.

To echo Einstein's comment at the beginning of this chapter, it's far more rewarding, for ourselves and others, to strive to be of value.

Einstein reportedly made that remark to a reporter not long before his passing in 1955. More specifically, his advice was directed to the reporter's son, a young man who accompanied his father to the interview and took the opportunity to ask the acclaimed physicist how he should live his life.

In stressing value, Einstein cautioned that life was not a question of being successful, of accumulating the most possessions or the biggest pile of money. It was not a matter of measuring success by how much you got out of life. Rather, a full life well lived was a matter of putting more into life than what you got out of it—your respect for and service to others, your commitment to high ideals, and your honesty and compassion. It is being the kind of person who lifts and inspires those around them.

That really stands the success versus failure dichotomy on its head. Instead of the struggle between winning and losing, it is far more meaningful to focus our efforts on what we bring to life—both our own and others'. Success and failure come and go, but value is far more permanent and impactful. And, as we've discussed, if you first value yourself, then it's possible to imbue everything you say and do with every bit as much value.

That's a life we can all strive for, far beyond the noise of success and failure.

....

"My mission in life is not merely to
survive, but to thrive; and to do so
with some passion, some compassion,
some humor, and some style."
—MAYA ANGELOU

....

CHAPTER 6

RAISE YOUR EXPECTATIONS

....

*"We are all in the gutter, but some
of us are looking at the stars."*
—OSCAR WILDE

....

To interpret Oscar Wilde's observation in the quote above, one of the greatest differentiators in how we live our lives is our level of expectation—what we truly think we are capable of accomplishing.

He certainly seems to suggest that even those of us in the most challenging, even discouraging, predicaments can benefit from raising our level of expectation. And, as we'll discuss shortly, that can come down to having a realistic, yet optimistic outlook on what you can achieve.

Unfortunately, not everyone understands the value of setting those sorts of challenging, yet attainable goals. One of the most heartbreaking things for me to witness are people who don't fulfill their potential. For me, unrealized promise for whatever reason represents a form of betrayal. Maybe a person is denied an opportunity to shine because of forces outside of their control. Sometimes, admittedly, it can come down to a case of bad luck.

But, as I see it, the most devastating cause of failed potential is self-inflicted. Failing to fulfill your potential as the result of other factors is devastating enough, but it's particularly shattering when it comes down to a lack of motivation, purpose, or commitment. As I alluded to in the prior chapter, that's a form of failure that can be rather difficult to learn from. Even failure isn't a sufficiently gifted teacher to improve someone who simply refuses to do the work.

I would like to share a story of a person who embodies this. She has struggled with her sense of worth since early childhood. We first met, when her parents and I were in graduate school together. Whenever she felt pressure to meet someone's expectations, fear would take over, her grades would suffer, and she would withdraw. During these times, she would give up and refuse to do anything. The fear of failing would paralyze her. Fortunately, her parents recognized that she needed help. With counseling from a behavioral specialist, she managed to overcome these demons and complete college. The counselor helped her discover the origins of this behavior and taught her strategies that changed her life. What if her parents didn't recognize this behavior in time? She would have continued to suffer internally, doubting her self-worth and value, running away from who she is. Just as important, due to the help she received, she was able to reset the expectations of herself. In discovering her internal power and agency, she was able to do the work that was desperately needed. Lacking that, the world would have missed out on the gifts she has to offer to society. I truly believe that she is poised to do great things because she possesses an underlying genius.

I am a mentor to a person who embodies this. She has struggled with her sense of worth since early childhood. Her parents shared a story about her disappearing during a family gathering. They started searching for her thinking she might have been abducted, only to find her hiding in the closet. The parents didn't think anything of it at the time. Their daughter was a perfect child until this behavior began to surface again—hiding during college. Whenever she felt pressure to meet someone's expectations, fear would take over and she would run away or simply disappear. She managed to complete college, but only because she received the appropriate counseling from a behavioral specialist. The counselor helped her discover the origins of this behavior and taught her strategies that changed her life.

What if her parents didn't recognize this behavior in time? She would have continued to suffer internally, doubting her self-worth and value, running away from who she is. Just as important, due to the help she received, she was able to reset her expectations of herself. Lacking that, the world would have missed out on the gifts she has to offer to society. I truly believe she is poised to do great things because she possesses an underlying genius.

The message is clear. Recognizing one's challenges, and being willing to face them head on, can make a tremendous difference in your life.

As no one less than Michelangelo suggested, the greater danger is not that your hopes are too high, and you fail to reach them; it's that they're too low and you do. I firmly believe that setting high expectations creates a mindset for achievement. It forces us to look at things greater than ourselves. These seemingly wild ideas of oneself and capabilities pushes us to be more, opening the door to a new world of possibilities. In doing so, we release the powerful being that resides in all of us. It unleashes a person with no limits, where we become the infinite being with infinite possibilities.

Don't be afraid to fail to reach your dreams. If this happens, it places you at a high vantage point to start again or pivot to something different—two choices that place you into a position for even greater achievement. It is the mindset of a successful person.

On the other hand, if we set our sights too low, we will never reach our true potential.

Now here comes the tricky part. Unrealized potential can also be due to the precise opposite: unrealistic expectations. However enviable it might seem, the belief that we can do anything we truly set our minds to simply isn't grounded in reality. It can be detrimental to our ability to grow into the person that we are truly to become.

When I was thirteen years old watching the Apollo 11 mission, I was thrilled by our landing on the moon. I decided that I wanted to be an astronaut. But the reality was, other than my ambition, I had neither the talent nor the skills to accomplish that goal. Even though I was capable, I was incapable of achieving that goal in my circumstances at that time. I had to honestly assess my position and then map out my path toward this objective.

We all have certain strengths or weaknesses. We can work diligently to be able to do all things well, but many things are beyond our physical, mental, and even emotional capacities. That's generally not a reflection on us—it's just the way things happen to be.

Moreover, just because we're incapable of doing something at a particular stage of our lives doesn't translate to an unalterable reality. Perspective and the possibility of growth are everything.

This all circles back to a recurring theme—the essential value of taking the time to know yourself. Part of that exploration can and should include an honest self-assessment of abilities and skills. Like other such forms of self-examination I've suggested previously, this can prove to be unnerving and even unpleasant. But, again, it's far too important to tackle with less than a completely candid attitude or, worse yet, to ignore completely.

It is from this vantage point that we can have the foundation to set realistic expectations for ourselves.

BE REALISTIC AND REALIGN

Self-understanding is key to setting realistic expectations. Having a genuine sense of what you're capable of carries a number of important benefits and advantages. For one thing, it gives you a clear sense of what you can do as well as those things that—at least for now—are not in your sweet spot. But, if you're aware of what you're not particularly adept at, you can set to work improving them. That's as much a part of realistic expectations as anything else—knowing what you have to do to improve within a realistic framework.

That carries significant ramifications for yourself as well as for others around you. With regard to yourself, you'll be grounded in reality. By knowing yourself, you're going to enjoy what you do well and apply yourself constructively to better whatever is beyond your reach at the moment. Not only does that position you to improve yourself, but you'll also be a happier person than someone who repeatedly struggles with challenges they can't overcome.

Just as important, you won't chronically sell yourself short. While attempting to achieve the impossible is maddening, aiming for goals that are well below your abilities is no less wasteful. As I alluded to earlier in this chapter, it's a form of self-betrayal—one of the most heartbreaking situations I can imagine.

One of my dear friends, whom I have watched all their life, is a prime example of selling yourself short. They were a very smart person; gifted, in fact. But, because of their gift, they always stay in trouble. They have had several run-ins with the law, from DUIs to unpaid parking tickets. (If you don't pay a simple parking ticket, and it happens a lot, the judge will issue a warrant for your arrest. I didn't know that until I was involved in bailing them out of jail on several occasions.) And each time, they would tell me they would never do it again. We would discuss the issue; they would get counseling and their behavior would improve, only to reoccur over and over again.

What is the definition of insanity? It is doing the same thing over and over again while expecting a different outcome.

The travesty is that this person is one of the smartest people I know. Without the aberrant behavior, on the surface they seem highly regarded and upstanding. This is what psychiatrists would call anxiety disorder coupled with depression. They are hiding in plain sight, but no one sees them except those of us close enough to know them. Because of their behavior, they have not become the person that they could be. They have set unrealistic goals and, in many cases, failed to achieve them, only to blame the people around them. This leads to disappointment, which literally drives them to drink and other negative behaviors that ultimately keep them in trouble. They were caught in a vicious cycle that feeds on itself. They sold themselves short by their behavior, which led them to trouble. The trouble then drives the narrative of failure—fueled, I believe, by fear. Their unwillingness to face the consequences and learn from their mistakes stunt their grow as an individual. It led to an unrealistic perspective of themselves and the world around them.

Addiction is real. It is a disease that plagues many families.

Having a realistic perspective of yourself also benefits those around you. If you are aware, you have room for improvement and you're open to input from others. You are eager to learn what others have to share to make you better.

SETTING REALISTIC EXPECTATIONS

The challenge (and opportunity) of establishing realistic expectations is akin to the question that young people ask me repeatedly—how do I know what I want out of life? Those two issues go hand in hand. If you know who you are, you will have the opportunity to discover what it is that you are meant to do in this world—a pretty enviable position in which to find yourself.

An anecdote from my childhood underscores this. When I was very young, I already knew that I was also good at drawing. Starting in kindergarten, armed with sketchpads, I began to draw different things at every opportunity. One recurring subject was spaceships, which I would draw repeatedly, adjusting features here and there, always imagining myself at the controls as I sped toward the moon or some other destination in space.

But other elements of my work were more earthbound. For instance, I loved to draw houses of various sizes, shapes, and features. It came quite naturally to me. I didn't have to teach myself to draw or take a class—I just seemed to be able to do it.

That set up something of a fork in the road by the time I reached high school. Fueled by experiences such as the one when I was in the high school band, I was giving some thought to going into medicine. On the other hand, since I liked drawing buildings, architecture was also naturally appealing. I realized I was also an innate builder.

This confluence left me with choices to make. On the one hand, I could become an architect. At the same time, the rewards of medicine were also very appealing. Adding to the mix, space travel captivated me, posing the options of astronaut and aerospace engineer. At the time, I decided to pursue aerospace engineering, where I could employ my drawing skills alongside my interest in space travel. But just as my mind was set on this path, with the end of the Apollo program, NASA laid off a large number of aerospace engineers.

Were those expectations realistic? In hindsight, they were, as my subsequent career supports. However, that event inevitably steered me toward medicine and space exploration without the architectural component. My point in sharing this experience is to highlight another element of self-knowledge: paying attention to your reactions to experiences as you proceed through life.

Treat your reactions as more meaningful than just an immediate response to something. Look at them as signs and guideposts. Pay attention to those reactions, because they can point you toward what you may truly be meant to be and what you can realistically aspire to. They can prove your earliest guides to setting goals that are attainable and, every bit as important, represent the fullest use of your skills and abilities.

Should you choose to pay sufficient attention to those reactions, you can avoid the tragic fate of far too many people who find themselves pursuing goals—a profession, for instance—that they truly do not embrace. Picture an adult working at a job who hears of someone else whose work genuinely sounds both challenging and engaging and thinks, "Gosh, I wish that was me." Of course, no matter where you are in your life, you can always try to pivot to pursue your true passion, but far too many of us settle for a status quo that's unfulfilling and below our capabilities. It is far better to be one of the lucky ones, such as me, who took note of my reactions fairly early in life.

Fortunately, though, our expectations don't need to be static or cast in stone. Since we are all continually growing and evolving, so, too, should our expectations of ourselves. As we grow, we gather more experience and, as a result, are often capable of far more than we might have been earlier in life. For instance, when I completed my training in aerospace medicine at the Brooks Air Force Base in San Antonio, Texas, I naturally emerged from the program with higher expectations than when I began. It enhanced my skills as a space clinician, researcher, and later as the Crew Medical Officer on my space flights. Having been challenged on all sorts of levels, I came to appreciate that I was capable of far more than I might have imagined only a short time prior.

But you must allow yourself the freedom to adjust your expectations. I can't stress this point enough. Establishing realistic expectations for yourself doesn't mean setting it and forgetting it. Once you have a goal in mind, it's not as though it can never be changed. You have to allow yourself the freedom, imagination, and even courage to adjust those expectations when you feel it's genuinely warranted. Never selling yourself short means being open-minded and receptive to the fact that you can accomplish more the more experience and insight you gain. Give yourself the leeway to make those sorts of beneficial revisions.

Lastly, don't limit expectations to your professional life. Our personal selves can also benefit enormously by watching our reactions to certain things. For instance, if you have an experience like mine in the high school band that I shared earlier—when someone had a heart attack and all I could do was wish I could help—it doesn't mandate a career in medicine and nothing else. If you've taken the time to know yourself, you may well realize that medicine is simply beyond your ability to pursue as a profession.

However, you can learn CPR or take a first-aid class. Those may not lead down a career path, but they can certainly prove rewarding on a personal, spiritual basis. And, who knows, the time may come when you can help someone in a medical situation. That can prove no less rewarding than a fully trained physician being of service to patients.

Hitting the sweet spot of realistic expectations—not too low but not unattainably high—is valuable. It is a difficult balance between setting high standards for yourself while at the same time measuring it against the realities of your innate abilities and those yet to be acquired. But there is one thing I know: most people set lower expectations than they are capable of. Don't be that person!

ATTITUDE DETERMINES ALTITUDE

At first glance, the phrase "attitude determines altitude" might seem to run counter to the prior discussion of being realistic when setting expectations. If you have a certain level of skill or ability, that would seem to pretty much dictate the remainder of the game. No amount of attitude can shift that reality, right?

Not quite. Granted, being realistic is an important byproduct of knowing yourself and, as a result, establishing attainable expectations and goals. But your attitude can also play a central role to what, in effect, turns out to be completely realistic.

Phrased simply, if your expectations are low, that's likely where you're headed. And attitude does, in fact, play a key role in setting expectations. If your goals are modest, you likely have a modest attitude as to what you may be capable of. That may be somewhat realistic, but it can also prove to be rather limiting.

But attitude can also serve to boost your expectations and horizons—it depends on the attitude you take regarding the experience. For instance, in the context of space exploration, you may be aiming for a distant star but, in the end, the farthest you can reach is the moon. If your attitude is anything short of getting to that star is a failure, then you're simply caught in the self-destructive trap of setting your expectations much too high.

However, if your attitude approaches the journey differently, the outcome may also feel completely different. True, you didn't make it to that star, but you did reach the moon. That's an achievement, something to be proud of. You have, in fact, achieved something of significance. It is also as every bit as valuable because it imbues you with the confidence to boost your expectations of yourself and what you can do. Next time, you may be able to get to that star that you couldn't reach the first time around.

This gives me an opportunity to brag about Valerie. All her life she has known that she loves being around people. As a teenager, she would host parties for her friends. Coming from a traditional middle-class family in Philadelphia, she reached out across socioeconomic boundaries to include all for her parties. I classify her as "social"—a standing joke between us. That means she will talk to anybody, anywhere. That is her gift.

After completing high school, Valerie attended Duke University, where she continued her "social work," becoming president of her class. From the influence of family and friends, she always thought that she would become a lawyer. But, after Duke, she interned at a law firm in Philadelphia—and hated it. The thought of reading briefs all day didn't fit into her social construct. She pivoted and decided to go into business. She joined an asset management firm but realized that she needed more training. So, she applied and was accepted to Wharton Business School, where she received an MBA. Shortly after completing her degree, she was interviewing for jobs and walked onto the bond trading floor of the firm, Salomon Brothers. It was loud, chaotic, and fun. It fit her personality perfectly. Finding her place enabled her to become one of the leading investors in fixed income investments for one of the largest firms in the country. In fact, Valerie was awarded the honor of being one of the top ten women on Wall Street. I am so proud of her!

Her success has been driven in large part by her positive attitude. This gift enabled her to succeed not only in her career but has influenced her life as well as the people who have been blessed to know her.

Attitude boosts the power of many forms of potential. If you approach a challenge with an all-or-nothing attitude, that leaves very little room for anything short of complete success or utter failure. Coming out on the short end of that dichotomy can be discouraging even to those of us who consider ourselves highly motivated.

On the other hand, if your attitude allows you to focus on and embrace whatever value you can derive from an experience, that's a form of growth that doesn't tip exclusively between success and failure. For instance, in my case, had I not been particularly adept at mathematics and science, my chances of becoming an astronaut would have been virtually nonexistent. But, if I nonetheless worked to improve my math and science abilities, they may well have benefitted me in some other field or application. It just may not have been in a job in outer space.

Attitude and reasonable expectations have a powerful synergy. If you have the attitude that emphasizes growth and improvement over winning or losing, you're likely to set and be comfortable with expectations that are within the realm of reality. But looking exclusively on success or failure often doesn't foster personal growth. For some, failure is devastating. Even if they do succeed, the only outcome to be fixed on is yet another form of success down the line that they may or may not achieve. It simply isn't very constructive.

And, speaking of constructive, setting realistic goals doesn't always mean you're going to enjoy whatever you have to do to reach a goal. As often as not, realistic expectations involve work and other activities that we may simply not like.

Here's a personal example. As a business and non-profit leader, I often have to deal with statistics in my work. Put simply, I hate it. In every field that I've been in—medicine, business, and space—I've had to deal with statistics. I do not enjoy working with it.

Yet I do work with it. I gut it out and do what I must do, because that's what I have to do to accomplish my goals. My attitude drives my ability to power through them. That makes my particular goals realistic since I'm willing to push through tasks and activities that I simply do not enjoy. Attitude empowers me to broaden goals that are, in fact, realistic because I recognize that not every step toward personal development is going to be pleasant or fun. Sometimes, it's real, grinding work. My attitude boosts my altitude because I am able to accept it.

ALIGN, DON'T RESIGN

Knowing how to set and live with realistic expectations can also be particularly valuable when fate and fortune take you in a different direction than you expected. If your goals are realistic and your path takes an unexpected or unwanted turn, an ability to ride that change rather than resist it can often be the most realistic and effective option. It's a question of aligning rather than resigning.

My early experience with the astronaut program offers an ideal example. When I was initially rejected for the astronaut corps, I could have given up completely and pursued something else—perhaps a field entirely outside of space travel. Instead, effectively embracing the rejection, I decided to accept the opportunity to work in space medicine. As such, I was aligning myself not merely to participate in groundbreaking work and research, but also positioning myself to be in an optimal spot when the time came to select the next astronaut class.

As a result of my willingness to align rather than resign, I was given an opportunity to do things that I would have never done otherwise. I would have never become an expert in the effects of space travel on bone. I would have never gone into the Air Force to become a flight surgeon, and, as a result, obtain important military training. I would have never even learned how to fly an airplane.

As it ultimately turned out, a willingness to align allowed me to experience things that, prior to that, I would never have even considered as vaguely realistic expectations. I had always had it in my head that I could become the first African American physician who also flew in space as an astronaut. What wasn't on my radar at the time was one of the ultimate experiences of my time as an astronaut—the opportunity to walk in space. Had I been accepted into that first class, I'm not so sure the stars would have been sufficiently aligned to make that happen.

As you can see, an ability to align doesn't mean a willingness simply to settle. Rather, it's repositioning, putting yourself in a slightly different angle to approach challenges and opportunities. In business, we call it a pivot. It means that when we find that a company's product or service is no longer relevant, we change direction. We look for other opportunities for different products. In your personal life, you're looking for opportunities to use your innate skills. If you've taken the time to get to know who you are and what you can achieve, a willingness to align and realign rather than resign can constantly raise the bar of realistic possibilities.

UNDERSTANDING THE "WHY"

It is most important to understand why you do things. I cannot emphasize this more. As part of your self-exploration and soul searching, you will come to know the "why" you do the things you do. In my description of my friend with depression and anxiety in the previous chapter, they never understood why they did the things they did. Despite seeing psychiatrists for their problems, they continued to struggle. I believe it was because they could never quite grasp the root cause of their condition. I will admit that in many cases, mental illness can prevent this discovery. But, understanding the why, the root causes of the issues, are at the heart of psychotherapy.

I was at a conference once where the organizer of the meeting opened the proceedings with this statement: "Before we can meet our challenges within this state, we must focus on the 'why' we are here. But most important is why you are here."

What a powerful overture for the audience to consider. Because the answers would be the foundation from which we would proceed, we would build our mission for the organization. It can also be the foundation for how you can live your life, how you can meet the challenges and struggles of your world. Each of us has our individual "crosses to bear," our goals to reach, and our dreams to fulfill. They can be mastered if we understand the why.

To pull it all together for me: When my parents divorced, I needed to understand the why. So, I spent a fair amount of time with both my parents, trying to understand their differences and their views. When I was in high school trying to decide on my vocation, I researched my choices, explored my feelings around those choices, and ultimately made one: to become a doctor and astronaut. My head decision became a heart decision because of the answers to the why.

Finding answers to the why defined my roadmap to most of the things that I have done and accomplished in life. You could do the same, too.

A PURPOSEFUL LIFE

I have always described myself as a physician, who became an astronaut, venture capitalist, and philanthropist. On the way to accomplishing those things, my life has been blessed. After medical school, I completed my residency in internal medicine at the Mayo Clinic, followed by a fellowship at NASA Ames Research Center, which led me to my career as a principal investigator, flight surgeon, and astronaut, flying two space shuttle missions. Following my space career, I wanted to explore another dream to build wealth. This idea came about from a

Black Economics class that I took at the University of Houston as an undergraduate. Our professor then had asked us a simple question: "Do you think that the plight of Blacks in America is a Black or White issue?"

This was in the seventies during the time of Black Power, soul/funk music, and the Black movement. In the class were a mix of races, Black, White, and Brown. He let the question hang in the air for us to discuss. In the end, the Black students blamed the Whites, the Whites blamed the Blacks, and the Brown were mostly neutral on the subject. After a fair amount of bickering, the professor made this statement.

"The plight of the African American is not a Black or White issue; it is green and gold. The success of the Black community depends on how we can obtain more money and build wealth."

From this simple discussion, my life was enhanced by another goal in life: To learn how to make money and grow wealth. Not just simple wealth, but generational wealth. I have always admired families like the Vanderbilts and the Kennedys. Their forefathers built lasting wealth. I wanted to do the same for my family.

So, in 2002, with the help of my new mentors Jack Gill and Robert Ulrich, managing partners at Vanguard Ventures, I launched Vesalius Ventures. For over twenty years now, we have invested in early- and mid-stage companies and entrepreneurs in the telemedicine space. Over that time, we have had winners and losers. Fortunately, we have had more winners than losers, which resulted in a highly successful venture capital business. I have been blessed to have fulfilled another goal of building generational wealth!

Since completing my residency at the Mayo Clinic, I have always practiced medicine. During my fellowship at the NASA

Ames Research Center in Moffett Field, California, I moonlighted at a local neighborhood clinic on the evenings and weekends. Later, when I joined NASA Johnson Space Center in Houston, Texas as a civil servant, I asked and received special approval to work outside of the government as a professor of family medicine at Baylor College of Medicine and professor of internal medicine at the University of Texas Medical Branch. I saw patients as a doctor. I am especially proud of my work in the community health clinic throughout the Houston area, providing indigent medical care.

After leaving the Astronaut Office, I chose to transition into business, fulfilling another dream from college, while also asking why communities of color are left behind. The answer to the why was not black or white, but green (meaning building wealth). Lastly, the answer to the "why" lead me to my work of giving back and philanthropy.

Along the way, I have been intentional in investing in my community through my family foundation. The Harris Institute/Foundation is a 501(c)(3), non-profit organization founded to serve socially and economically disadvantaged communities locally and across the nation striving to reach the most underserved populations in the areas of education, health, and wealth. We utilize the "Pillars of Success" to empower students and communities throughout the nation and the world. The Harris Institute/Foundation was established to advance the mission of creating community-based initiatives that (1) enhance the quality of education, (2) improve health and well-being, and (3) create and sustain wealth. We empower individuals, minorities, and others who are underserved, underrepresented, and/or socioeconomically disadvantaged to recognize their potential and pursue their dreams. Its initiatives are administered by

The Harris Foundation, Inc., through the creation of innovative programs.

Through "Policies in Action," we are addressing critical issues facing the US and developing programs for change. We have served more than 1 million students since 1998.

Giving back to my community and to my country is of tremendous importance to me. I believe in the edict "To whom much is given, much will be required" (Luke 12:48) King James version. President John F. Kennedy said it differently in 1961: "To whom much is given much is required." Of course, he was referencing the Bible as he talked about the qualities of great leadership.

When we have been blessed with abilities, talents, wealth, knowledge, time, and I would add, opportunity, it should not only benefit ourselves but others, too.

No matter what you do, the only thing that matters is that you do it with a "good heart" and pay it forward to set the foundation for the next generation. Out of the things that a person does during this short life, I believe that the great investment is how we give back.

Discovering your meaning and understanding the "why" is critical to developing your skills and talents. Out of this comes a fruitful and fulfilling life. It will lead you to your passion, and your passion will guide you toward your destiny. Hopefully, this destiny will be the fulfillment of your purpose in life. After all, we were all born for a reason. What is yours?

CHAPTER 7

YOUR UNLIMITED POTENTIAL

....

"Continuous effort—not strength or intelligence—is the key to unlocking our potential."
—WINSTON CHURCHILL

....

INFINITE BEING WITH INFINITE POSSIBILITIES

I have been to Dubai, United Arab Emirates (UAE) numerous times. Each time, I have had a different experience. Once I was there for the Arab Health Conference and exhibition, one of the world's largest healthcare meetings. People and companies travel from all over the world to show their wares in that event. I was there to look for opportunities in telemedicine, as I believed that the region was ripe for the use of technology for the delivery of healthcare.

A beautiful country, the UAE was a desert with nomadic tribes and fishing villages until a man with a vision came along.

His name was Sheikh Zayed bin Sultan Al Nahyan, the founder of the UAE. He served as president of the UAE since the formation of the Federation on December 2, 1971, and as ruler of the Emirate of Abu Dhabi since 1966. When oil was discovered in the UAE, he began to lay out a vision that would change the face of the country. Once a fishing village, Dubai has been transformed into one of the world's most progressive and modern cities. It is becoming the financial center of the Middle East, rivaled only by Saudi Araba and Qatar.

Every great accomplishment of society has been championed by a person with vision, one who looks at the world differently and sees something no one else has. This vision is something that great CEOs have, too. Consider Steve Jobs at Apple, Bill Gates and Steve Ballmer of Microsoft, Larry Page and Sergey Brin of Google, Kenneth Chenault of American Express, and Richard Dean "Dick" Parsons of Citi Group/AOL/Time Warner. Add to that list Sheryl Sandberg of Facebook and Ursula Burns of Xerox and VEON, and Robert Smith of Vista Equity Partners. And of course, we have the next generation of CEOs— Thasunda Brown Duckett, president and chief executive officer of TIAA, and Rosalind G. Brewer, former CEO of Walgreens Boots Alliance.

The challenge is to find that visionary within you—a daunting task for most of us. We have been told "no" for so long we have incorporated the word into our being. It defines us. It limits us and dictates who we are. I know this because I have been a victim of its effect. My task and yours is to liberate ourselves from those things and people who hold us back and transform the "no" mindset into one of "Yes, I can." Does it work? For sure. One example of changing a mindset into the "Yes, we can!" movement is President Barack Obama. It was his rallying cry during his campaign for office. Obviously, words and thoughts are a powerful tool for achievement and, as we can see, it can even lead to attaining the presidency of the US.

WHERE DO YOU START?

Start by making up your mind to do something. Decide to step out onto a limb. Take a chance to think differently if your mindset is limited. It doesn't matter what it is, as long it takes advantage of your God-given gifts. The well-kept secret is that when we find our passion and our vision, we enable the higher power that, in turn, enables our goals or dreams. We become the very thing that we have been seeking our entire life. When discovered, there is great joy in accomplishment.

The first time I discovered this self-empowerment was when I was fifteen. During that time, we lived in small community called Tohatchi, New Mexico. It was a time of transition for my family. My mother had remarried, changing the dynamic of our family. My stepfather and mother decided that it was time for us to move back to Texas. They chose San Antonio, as they both had jobs waiting there. Plans had been put in motion, but with one problem… me. I was excited about moving back to Texas, but I wanted to do it as a licensed driver. In New Mexico, you could get your license at fifteen—Texas set it at sixteen.

Being fifteen, getting my driver's license was one of the many things that meant the world to me. If I could move to Texas being able to drive, it would boost my standing with the kids in my new high school. I struck a deal with my mother. If I could find a driver's education class that could be completed in the time before we left, they would support it. That gave me only two months, not a lot of time to find an opening in a course, take it, and apply for a license. So, I went to work. Within a couple of weeks, I was enrolled in a six-week driving course in Gallup, New Mexico, about thirty minutes from home. I successfully completed the course and applied for the license with only a few weeks left to spare before leaving for Texas. Two months after arriving in San Antonio, I received my license in the mail. It was a miracle!

No, not a miracle, actually. It was me setting a goal, holding that idea in my head and being willing to work hard to accomplish it. I wasn't willing to take no for an answer. I was determined to make "Yes, I can" the only option if I was going to be successful. In my mind, there was no room for failure. It was my first lesson on how to succeed in life and the impact that individual power can have on the world around me.

Despite the trials and tribulations of life, we should all be grounded in this fact of life—the fact that we are infinite beings with unlimited power that is ours if we choose to use it. We need to keep this notion in mind.

But I also recognize that there can be obstacles to the visioning process. I have had these challenges myself. Every time I fail, it takes a toll on the vision that I have of myself. I look around and wonder what others think. Sometimes I fall victim to my self-doubts and disappointment for failing. I replay the loss in my head. I see myself as a failure, unworthy of consideration. Why didn't I do better? Who am I? What value am I bringing to the world? Am I not important (or not as important as others)?

In my senior year at the University of Houston, I was preparing to go to medical school. After all the hard work of being a premed student, as I previously mentioned, I applied to six medical schools in Texas, received interviews at all, but was only accepted to one. The process was painful, especially for me. It lasted about six months, including the application itself, the interviews, and waiting on the decision of the selection commit-tee. I recall being so disappointed by all the rejection letters that I received. I began to develop an alternative strategy—perhaps I could work in a lab, do research, or go to graduate school? I was beginning to question my work, my credentials, and even my worth. I was beginning to feel sorry for myself during my times of self-reflection. During one of the few times that I communi-cated with my biological father, he encouraged me to hang in there and offered a prayer to console me.

Just when all hope was gone, I received a letter from Texas Tech University School of Medicine, in all places...Lubbock. The only thing I knew about Lubbock was that it was home of the Red Raiders and for Black people surrounded by massive cotton fields. And I was going to medical school here. I received a call from Jim Bob Jones, Dean of Students, to welcome me to the class of 1978. I was going to be a doctor! It was something that I had desired since being inspired by my family physician in San Antonio, Dr. Frank Bryant, and my quest to become an astronaut, following in the footsteps of NASA's astronaut ranks that included Dr. Joseph Kerwin, the first American physician to travel in space. My ambition had now set me on the path to take my first steps. These steps would, over time, test my resolve. In this case, my doubts were overcome by my desire, hard work, and faith.

OVERCOMING DOUBT

I have doubted myself and my worth during several key times in my life, particularly during medical school. During those times, I had thoughts of being a failure. These are thoughts that we may have had in various situations. For some of us, it leaves us so disappointed and distracted that we contemplate withdrawing from the world in solitude. Others may become so distraught that they lose sight of the pleasures of life.

Remember it takes courage to live with failure and work to overcome it. Don't give up on yourself and life. Courage is facing your failure, your mistakes, and your challenges, and remaining committed to overcoming them. You will survive. You will make it. You will move on. In so doing, you will grow, becoming stronger and offering an example for others who find themselves in similar predicaments.

Overcoming doubt in our life requires vigilance on our part. We must recognize this for what it truly is—a lifelong struggle. Adopting strategies to help us cope is critical to not only surviving but thriving.

My strategy involves recognizing my unique place in the universe. Part of that for me was my discovery of the path toward God. I believe that our purpose lies in becoming all that we can be within the constraints into which we are born. In overcoming those constraints, we grow to become the very thing that we seek. As a result, we are in a better position to help others in their own quest. There is an overall purpose; in growth, we become more like God, taking our rightful place as co-creators of our world. You become the power that Christ, the Buddha, Mohammad, and others sought.

This will probably be one of the most difficult things that you will do in life, but it must be done, sooner or later. By accepting your place and role in the universe, you become the thing you seek. This order will translate into peace and joy for you and everyone with whom you come into contact.

BEING FEARLESS

Even though I have been a seeker of truth and knowledge, I have not always been fearless in my approach to life. I can only imagine what I could have accomplished if I had been. When I think of this, I am reminded of the verses in the Bible and self-help books that talk of success and achievement in life. The Bible talks of the power of faith. Norman Vincent Peale wrote about the power of positive thinking. Many speak of the unlimited power of the human being.

As stated before, I began my search for meaning early in life, after we arrived in the Navajo Nation. I sat on our apartment steps, staring off into the distant valley and mountain range in the background, contemplating my world. My first question was: Who am I? From the media of the day, I was defined a "Negro" or "colored kid," whose options at the time were limited. In the sixties, there were set norms for our society. It said that if you were White, your place was on top; if you were Black, the expectations were lower. But there were men and women who began to resist that narrative: Dr. Martin Luther King Jr., Malcom X, John Lewis, Angela Davis, Maya Angelou, Shirley Chisholm, Katherine Johnson, Dorothy Vaughan, and Mary Jackson (the last three of *Hidden Figures* fame).

With the help of these great men and women, we began to see ourselves differently. The demand for human rights and voting rights became louder. I saw this as a kid and realized that I indeed had a bright future if I only chose to pursue it. I decided to believe what my mother, my family, and my friends saw in me: "A soul capable of great things." One of those great things was this notion that I could become an astronaut. I had let go of fear and doubt and accepted what life had in store for me.

GEORGE FLOYD

Despite my newfound power, the struggle for many of us remains. The murder of George Floyd in May 2020 changed the narrative of race in this country and around the world. It wasn't the first time that a Black man had been killed by the police. Nor was it the first time that it had been seen on television. As the nation had been seeing these images for years, it had become numb to this type of violence toward Black people. It was just accepted by all, even by Blacks. This was and is our lot in life—or at least in this country.

Why was the death of George Floyd different? What made the murder of this human being different from all the others? Historians and philosophers will be writing about this for decades to come. In my opinion, Floyd became an iconic symbol of suffering not only for Blacks in this country but for all people of color and those who have been oppressed. For the first time, the vicious act could be seen over and over again through multiple media outlets, with commentary not only from the mainstream news media, but by individuals via social media. The visibility was that much greater, as was the resulting dialogue.

Additionally, those images could truly be seen for what they were—a real-time execution of a human being. There was no covering it up. It became a symbol, where a White man could kill a Black person on national television. Even Whites seeing this cruel act were appalled. There was no doubt as to what they saw. Even though some conservative networks tried to change the narrative, the facts couldn't be altered. Some tried to justify the killing, saying that he had it coming because of his questionable background. It had worked in the past. This time, that argument fell flat, because the facts of the matter were visible to all who looked and honestly acknowledged the truth of what they saw.

This opened the Pandora's box for the discussion of systemic racism. Shortly after these events, several of my White colleagues and friends asked me to share my thoughts on racism and, more importantly, how they might address it personally and in their companies. I spent hours discussing my personal experiences and the impact that systemic racism had on my life. I shared the many things that I had to deal with as a Black man in this country, talking about what it was like to grow up in the US. I highlighted my experiences—both good and bad—in my pursuit for excellence, while overcoming the inherent prejudice growing up Black in this country. These struggles were real. And they remain real today.

BLACK IN AMERICA

As a Black man in America, I have always known that I must be twice as good to achieve half the success of my White counterparts. I now know that it applies to dark-complexioned people around the world as well. Why is it that the "haves" always think ill of the "have-nots" and then stereotype them as inferior because of their station and/or the color of their skin?

This need to dominate others has haunted the human race since the beginning of man's ascension on Earth. When will this dance stop and we can be seen as human beings with the same desires and ambitions for life? Why can't we find a common ground where we assist each other to obtain our individual desires and dreams?

I was once asked to serve on a panel to discuss systemic racism and its impact on society. Several notable figures joined me during the Zoom meeting. I shared a story of growing up in the 1960s during the civil rights movement, watching what was happening around me. One of the initiatives born from that movement was affirmative action. That was supposed to correct the wrongs and provide a way to promote economic and education advancement for all, particularly for African Americans.

Over the course of its implementation, the effort was taken up by other groups looking for their rights too—women, the LGBTQ+ community, immigrants, and others. As a result, the initiative whose purpose was to assist Black people in the US eventually shifted from the group for which it was originally intended. What do I mean by intended? Slavery in all its forms was a system that enslaved a group of people with the intent to support the growth of the nation. It worked too well. Unfortunately, it resulted in a class of privileged people and a subclass of disenfranchised ones. It was an intentional goal and extremely effective in its results, leaving an indelible impact on all those involved.

That was more than sixty years ago. It is no wonder that this country is still dealing with the aftermath of slavery because we have never dealt with its consequences.

This is at the core of systemic racism. It is a system where the haves do not want to give up power and the have-nots are locked in a fight for the right to simply enjoy the same access to the American Dream. And now with the influx of a new generation of immigrants, the tension between the competing groups is growing worse. I believe if this isn't addressed, it will be the death of our nation and democracy as we know it.

Today, we are living in dangerous times when the country is divided by class, race, ethnicity, sex, and gender identity. I do not believe there has ever been this much strife in this nation and, in fact, around the world. We are so divided. And this is played out daily in the media. We are a polarized nation, where our need to protect ourselves dictates how we see the world.

I am certainly no exception. My world is colored by my upbringing, my past, and my experiences. I recognize that I bring this bias with me wherever I go. The best that any of us can do is to be mindful, to be aware of how these feelings and emotions impact our decision-making. I am convinced that once we know who we are and how we react to our external environment, we can change our perspective to make better choices in life.

VERY FEW PEOPLE OF COLOR

Upon moving on from my time as an astronaut in 1996, I joined SpaceHab, a private space company, translating the work that I had been doing for NASA to the private sector. I spent three years at the company before I realized that NASA was not ready for the privatization of the space industry. So, I left SpaceHab to work in the venture capital business. I had no experience but was lucky enough to join one of the leading VC firms in the country—Vanguard Ventures, based out of Silicon Valley in Palo Alto, California; the home of the VC industry.

After a couple of years being mentored by Jack Gill and Robert Ulrich, general partners in the firm, I decided that I would start my own VC company. Vanguard agreed to become the lead investor of a syndicate of other investors, including Sevin Rosen, Fremont Ventures, and Boston Scientific. It took me two years to pull this group together, and we launched the firm in 2002.

What caught my attention was, for several years, I didn't see any fund managers who looked like me. It would take about four years before I saw anyone of color in the business. It wasn't until I was introduced to the National Association of Investment

Companies (NAIC) did I meet a small group of minority managers. When I talked with them, they all had the same story—how very difficult it was for them to raise capital to start their firms. We had similar stories of "headwinds" in starting our firms instead of the "tailwinds" that others seemed to have. This is with managers of color who came from top financial firms with outstanding track records that are attributed to them. And yet, these managers struggled to raise capital from the very firms where they were clearly successful. Why?

According to a 2021 Knight Foundation report, the overall percentage of assets under management controlled by diverse-owned firms was only 1.4 percent.[6] Despite some recent marginal progress, there remains a significant gap in this industry.

Despite seeing the data, many still argue that there is no systemic racism in the US and that Critical Race Theory (CRT) is putting forward a false narrative about the origin of racism. In fact, I was in a meeting recently where I heard a very wealthy person say publicly that he believed there was no systemic racism in the US at all. He said that everyone has the opportunity to succeed. I would agree with that if I weren't a victim of it myself and if everyone truly had equal opportunity.

In lieu of agreeing, my response is in the form of a question: Why do we have such a discrepancy in wealth in this country between Black, Brown, and White? What explains it? Some might argue that the difference is "their" abilities versus "ours." Others might say that the Black race is simply inferior.

At this point, I will simply leave the answer for you. Is that really true? I believe that history proves otherwise.

---

[6]   Hamlin, Jessica, "The Asset Management Industry Continues to Struggle with Diversity," Institutional Investor, December 10, 2021.

THE EXPECTATION OF COLOR AND SEX

I have been very fortunate to have had several lives. By that I mean I've been blessed to be a part of several professions in my short time here on Earth, where I have served in different roles as senior manager, director, vice president, president, and CEO. I have been involved in math and science education for more than twenty-five years through my philanthropy as president and founder of the Harris Institute/Foundation. I also served for more than twenty years as the managing partner of Vesalius Ventures, a venture capital firm that invests in early- to mid-stage healthcare technologies and companies. I was responsible for managing a portfolio of private assets of early- and mid-stage venture investments and operating companies. Lastly, I have had the honor to serve on the boards of directors for a variety of both non-profit and for-profit companies, as well as various roles in science, technology, engineering, and health organizations.

Even with all this experience and expertise, I sometimes find my background and knowledge being questioned in different settings. There is a different expectation for me and others like me. Why? Is it the color of my skin? Is it the dynamics of diversity, that complicates how I am being seen by society?

I have talked about this with many other Black and women executives who have had similar experiences in leadership. The only conclusion that one can come to is that we are treated differently because we are seen differently. The same is true for other people of color. When how people are treated are so subtle that they are unrecognizable by those in power, it undermines the hope of those who seek to be part of the American Dream. If we don't acknowledge these differences and seek to embrace them, it will have a powerful negative impact on our society.

BEING A BLACK LEADER

This dynamic also bleeds over to leadership. Being a Black leader in this country is undeniably challenging. Once you rise to the level of the CEO, you immediately have a target on your back. You're expected to do more. For society, you are an exception and a "credit to your race." You now represent an entire group of people. As a result, the things you do or don't do reflect on all other Black people, not just yourself.

A prime example of this was the rise of President Obama. When he hit the political scene, he was hailed as a savior for Black people, an example of what was possible for the underserved. When it became clear that he was the candidate to beat, he became a target. He took shots from the left and right—even from his own race. When he won the election, there was immediate admiration, followed by an even larger target landing squarely on his back, particularly from the right. And when there was no "dirt" to be found on him, things were invented, such as the question of his birthplace.

Some would say this is simply politics. I would say, yes, it is a question of politics, and of race.

As Black leaders, we face daily challenges to our authority from all sides. Again, we cannot make a mistake because it won't be forgiven. The bar is raised to a level far above others in the same role. That may sound bitter, but I know what I and others have experienced. That's the reality of this nation and of the world for people of color.

BEING WOKE

What does being "woke" mean? I don't believe that anybody really knows. It means different things to different people. For me, it means being conscious of who you are, being awake to your truth and those around you. It should be everyone's goal in life. Knowing your truth enables you to charge ahead fearlessly into the world that is yours to discover, to know your strengths and weaknesses for growing as a human being and as a person who is authentically themselves.

Being my authentic self has led me to confronting my Blackness and the anti-Blackness. Being woke to this reality is important for me. Unfortunately, that term, "being woke," has been co-opted into something negative although its original intention was positive.

Blacks in this country have suffered from unimaginable torture and death for more than three hundred years of slavery and oppression. Imagine if you were taken from your home and loved ones, placed in chains on ships where hundreds of thousands would eventually die on the journey, and arrive in a foreign land where you were forced to work as the mechanism that drove economic prosperity for others. If it weren't for the slave industry in this country and many others, they would not have risen to become the leading economies of the world. The US and other countries owe Black people a great debt.

Instead, we were given our freedom only to be marginalized and victimized through systemic racism. For many years, most people only paid attention when forced to—the civil rights marches of the fifties and sixties, the Voting Rights Act of 1965, affirmative action programs that enable many of us to simply get a fair chance to show what we can do. We are currently at an inflexion point in this country where we can empower those who have been suppressed to contribute to this nation once again. If we are only given a chance, we and the nation can reap the benefits of engaging all people in the American Dream.

In my self-reflection, I realized that I have an insatiable drive to be different from how some of those around me see me. Accordingly, I decided long ago that I would not buy into those stereotypes and that I would prove them all wrong for me and my race. In this discovery, I am loving who I am.

Whether you are Black, White, or Brown, knowing who you are, being who you are and loving who you are is critical to setting the foundation for your growth and discovering your unlimited potential. This statement also refers equally to gender, sex, and any other discriminator.

MY UNLIMITED POTENTIAL (AND YOURS)

Recognizing unlimited potential is a journey of self-discovery. Self-discovery can be painful yet necessary. Knowing who you are, understanding your place in the world, and acknowledging your own personal and cultural struggles are part of the foundation of accessing your full potential.

The title of this chapter is "Your Unlimited Potential." So, why did I spend time discussing race and systemic racism? Because, for me, the discovery of my unlimited potential came about through my journey as a Black person in the US. As I described in my first book, as a kid who had decided to become an astronaut, "I was an observer of the two continuing stories of that time: the space race with Russia and the race between two Americas." Sometimes it takes adversity to create that spark in one's soul. For me, it was my internal and external struggles that made me find ways to lift my spirits in an environment that repeatedly told me that I was "less than." I had to find ways to tap into the unlimited power of the individual God that resides in each of us.

Since many issues for Blacks in this country remain, I can only conclude that the only way in which Blacks are going to have true affirmative action in this country and around the world is through our own affirmative action—the initiatives and actions that promote Black economic power and the growth of wealth in underserved communities. And in doing so, we inherently strengthen the US.

For me, the revelation of my uniqueness and my innate talents drove me to become an achiever, seeking the highest person that I could be. In doing so, I realized that I am an infinite being with infinite possibilities. You can achieve the very same thing, but the journey is an internal one.

My travels in space gave me a different perspective. Even though I am a Christian and believed in God prior to leaving the planet, seeing the Earth from space imbued God with a much deeper layer of meaning. Visiting various places around the world has also reinforced the value of perspective. We cannot change the cards we are dealt, just how we play the hand. I used the hand that I was dealt. My challenges in life enabled my growth and the development of skillsets that I could have never imagined. It became the fuel that powered my ascension into space. Discovering something bigger than yourself has a way of changing the way you see things, no matter where you happen to be at the time. Keep watching for those opportunities to change and broaden your perspective, requires a continuous effort in unlocking our potential.

CHAPTER 8

QUESTION PERFECTION, ACCEPT IMPERFECTION

*"This is the very perfection of a man,
to find out his own imperfections."*
-SAINT AUGUSTINE>

"I am perfectly imperfect," someone once said to me.

That may not seem like an Earth-shattering proclamation, but it is to me. After all, it has taken me many years to be able to say it.

The previous chapter discussed the importance of setting reasonable expectations—not so low that you're effectively cheating yourself, but not so lofty either as to be unreachable.

That segues to a discussion of perfection. To me, perfection is a poison that can infect your soul. It's not necessarily because perfection is virtually impossible to attain, which it certainly is. Rather, it's because pursuing perfection, however understandable it might be, is like being on a treadmill. You can run until your lungs explode, but you never "get" anywhere. That's because perfection is a constantly moving target, one that slips further away every time we feel we're getting closer to it.

And, as it turns out, you're not running to try to catch perfection. Rather, perfection is running you.

Escaping from that dangerous habit can prove enormously beneficial to a far healthier goal—becoming all that you can be while accepting your flaws at the same time.

"MADE" TO BE PERFECT

If perfection is the destructive force that it is, it's really surprising that so many of us pursue it, nonetheless. Why? Well, in my case, I was made that way.

I've detailed the uncertainty and pain that often characterized my childhood. My first "injury" came with my parents' divorce. Just when I thought all was well, my mother decided to escape the pain of their marriage. As a six-year-old, I couldn't fathom their suffering. I was devastated by the departure of my dad. He was my world. Why would my mother leave him?

I later came to understand the truth that he was an alcoholic who, at the time, didn't know how to take care of his family. The loving man who kept insisting that he would get the family back together was never there. I wouldn't see him again until I graduated from high school, some twelve years later.

It was just the start of a confusing and volatile period in my life. As we moved from Temple, Texas, to Greasewood, Arizona, and later Tohatchi, New Mexico, my behavior and personality developed to protect myself. In effect, I created a persona of strength and confidence to hide the lingering fear and uncertainty of my life.

I use the word "persona" to make the point that we all create ways to protect ourselves from the outside world and all those secret fears we have (a psychiatrist I know refers to them as "ghosts" from our childhood). In my case, my persona focused on expanding my knowledge, intellect, and skills. It was a natural fit, as I was inherently smart and inquisitive.

On the one hand, it served me well. I was driven to become a high achiever. That certainly worked out—I became a medical doctor and an astronaut, and succeeded in the business world. Regarding medicine and space travel, those are two fields where perfection is a desirable goal—or, at the very least, as close to perfection as possible.

But, in my case and countless others, that sort of goal orientation inevitably leads to trying to capture perfection. The thinking is that, in order to succeed—and, as a result, become a truly worthwhile person—you've got to be perfect in how you execute. And that goes for everything.

That's what makes perfectionism a disease, a poison. For one thing, as I've stated, it truly is unattainable. In attempting to reach perfection, we inevitably fail. If you tie your sense of self-worth and value to perfection, you're destined to be bitterly disappointed, not to mention critical of yourself for failing to achieve such a noteworthy goal. For some of us, it's a constant ache that never goes away.

MAGNIFICENT DESOLATION

Insidious as it is, perfectionism can infect any of us. That goes as well for people whom you would think have little left to prove in their lives. In fact, one such example is a colleague of mine— Buzz Aldrin, one of the three crew members on the Apollo 11 mission that made the first successful trip to the moon.

Buzz is an icon. Not only is he a history-setting space explorer, but he's also a published author, the recipient of the Presidential Medal of Freedom, and an ongoing advocate for expanded space exploration. With a resume like that, one would think that he wouldn't have any issues.

He wrote about his life in the book *Magnificent Desolation: The Long Journey Home from the Moon*. The title was derived from his experience after his historic mission and return to Earth. He was asked the question that we as astronauts are all asked: "What was it like (in his case) to be on the moon?" Buzz famously expressed it as "magnificent desolation." In his mind, there were no other words to describe this life-altering experience.

In the book, he shares the heartbreak of losing his parents. In fact, his mother, Marion, battled with depression and committed suicide in May 1968—the year before Apollo 11. Her father (Buzz's grandfather) suffered from mental illness and also committed suicide.

Can you imagine the dynamics growing up in that household? Even though he and I never talked about his childhood, it had to be tough for him. Later on, at the peak of his career, he lost both his parents. Buzz also openly describes his own trouble with depression and alcoholism. He believes that he inherited depression from his family.

Depression and alcoholism impact many families in the US, including mine. Our only hope is that we become of aware of our individual challenges, personal and otherwise, use them as a stepping stone to a higher plane of existence, where we recognize the things that we need to work on and are willing to ask for help for things out of our control. None of us will get out of the world unscathed. Buzz Aldrin remains one of my heroes.

TO BE YOUNG AND DRIVEN

As I mentioned, Buzz's story, while certainly unique given the circumstances, is by no means completely unusual. Although those conditions can have a litany of causes, it's not hard to speculate that there could have been this need for perfection that may have contributed to the celebrated and challenging parts of his life. In some ways, his story embodied the factors that can lead to the struggle for perfection and the drive to achieve.

In chatting with some of my colleagues recently, I made a comment about how valuable it can be to be introspective. Now in my sixties, I'm certainly more thoughtful and reflective than when I was younger.

However, when you're young and driven to achieve, your foremost concern has nothing to do with the dangers of trying to reach perfection. Instead, you're far more focused on checking all the boxes—advancing in your career, earning recognition, starting a family, and accumulating wealth. With all that on the table, you don't have time to think about the underlying reasons why you're doing it. You just do it and, if your background and personality are aligned accordingly, you pursue it with every ounce of energy and dedication.

What you choose to pursue on your route to perfection reflects who you are and the influences of your upbringing. In my case, the break-up of my family, growing up in environments where I was more of an outsider than I might have been elsewhere, and other issues steered me toward fields where I could employ my intellect to its fullest. Further, I became involved in the "no nonsense, just give me the facts and let me make a decision" type of settings, such as medicine and space travel. Know what's involved, devise a strategy, and stick to the plan.

But it's essential to ultimately transition away from that narrow, highly-driven focus and realize that none of us can reach perfection. In its own way, it's liberating to realize that the chase for perfection inevitably leads to diminishing returns—the more we struggle to be perfect, the further away from it we can feel.

ALWAYS THE "BROWN SPOTS"

The effects of pursuing perfection go beyond how we are in our professional lives. It can also impact how we act in personal relationships—and often not always for the better.

Valerie tells me repeatedly about my fixation on the "brown spots." By that, she means, when she looks at a plant, she sees the lovely, vibrant green color. I, on the other hand, am inevitably drawn toward the plant's flaws and discolorations—the brown spots.

I do that because of who I am and what I've been trained to do. As a doctor, I can often tell what the issue is when a patient first walks into the examining room. Years of experience have taught me to observe how they stand, sit, talk, and, from there, devise an initial diagnosis. I just do it naturally and instinctively.

While that can be a great attribute for a physician, it's not quite so effective in other areas. Relationships are an ideal example. My habit of watching for particular signs—others' "brown spots"—can often lead to snap judgments, skepticism, and being critical of others. More often than not, I will act on those, unfortunately.

One time, I was on a flight somewhere. I watched a man board the aircraft, walking up the aisle as he looked for space in the overhead bins for his bag. I could tell he was a little annoyed because there wasn't a lot of unused space. He approached the flight attendant with his concerns. After a few minutes, he sat down next to me. I said to myself, "Oh boy, this is going to be a fun ride for the next five hours, trapped next to this whiner all the way from San Francisco to Washington, DC." Before a single word came out of his mouth, I had already summed him up as self-absorbed and arrogant. I was bracing myself.

Still, as he sat down, I said hello and he responded in kind. It turned out that it was the beginning of a wonderful dialogue. We talked the entire flight. He was the senior director for a large company, with tons of experience dealing with people from all walks of life. He had a very giving and open personality. He was a fan of space exploration, too. He was nothing like I had sized him up to be. We now serve on a non-profit board together and are changing lives for the better. This would have never happened if I had listened to my initial assessment. Further, I have learned a great deal from people despite what my preconceived notions of them might have been.

It's a case of the old glass half-full/half-empty quandary. My background and training have crafted my attention to focus on that part of the glass that's not full. Again, it's an important skill for a doctor, but decidedly less so outside of the medical setting. I have had to teach myself to pause when I am quick to judge. I learned to look at the situation or person differently…and if I see it as half-full, consider how I can contribute to fill it up.

THE SOLUTION: YOU ARE ENOUGH!

An obsessive drive to be perfect can also be tied to our attitude about self-worth. We have all experienced moments where we are in a situation or place or we are with someone who leaves us feeling that we are lacking in some way. Whether it's a matter of doing more or of somehow being more, we all have times where we feel as though we simply don't fit in, that we're not up to the situation or circumstances. Here's an example of what I mean.

As an astronaut, I spent a year in basic training where we were taught all things about space and how to survive in harsh environments. We went to flight school, underwent parachute training, survival courses (land and sea) and studied other relevant courses for the job. Most people in my class were military officers, many with prior flight training. I, on the other hand, had my pilot's license but only for single engine prop aircraft. I had obtained my pilot's license as part of my preparation to apply to become an astronaut. But when I arrived at Ellington Airfield in Houston, Texas, and looked at the plane that we were going to be learning to fly, I realized that what I did before wasn't enough.

First up was the classroom portion called "ground school." This is where you learn the basics of flight and all aspects of flying the T-38 jet aircraft. The T-38 is the workhorse of the Air Force and NASA. It is used for training Air Force pilots prior to stepping up to the F-16, F-18, and now the F-35 aircraft. For NASA, it's our main mode of training and transportation. You cannot become an astronaut without becoming proficient in it.

I got through the T-38 ground school with flying colors (no pun intended) but flying itself was an entirely different story. I was used to flying planes like the Cessna 210, whose top speed was 90 mph. The T-38 was more than nine times as fast—with a top speed of 858 mph! Things happen a lot faster at those speeds. Not only do you have to fly the plane, but you have to work the radios talking to ATC (air traffic control) and navigate, all at the same time. I was in way over my head. It was essentially a refresher for most of my colleagues with prior flight training, but for me, it was one of the biggest challenges of my life. After struggling to keep up and initially failing, I began to doubt my ability to make it. It felt like I was not fitting in. I was not up to the tasks at hand.

Where does this doubt come from? We are not born this way. God didn't have us enter this world with insecurities and fear. We were born with unlimited potential and the power to be more than we are at this moment. This is called growth. We are evolving creatures with an inquisitive nature. Our purpose in life is to explore our limits, whether that's striving for internal mastery or for an external purpose and position.

When it came to learning to fly, I needed to grow. I had to find the internal strength to say that I could do it. Even though many of my colleagues were soaring, I just needed more time—and more effort and experience. Fortunately, one of my flight instructors took a liking to me and helped me master the skills that I needed to become a jet pilot (or in the case of mission specialist, a co-pilot.) Thus began a whole series of successes in the astronaut program, highlighted by becoming one of the first astronauts in my class to be selected for a mission.

At this point, I had mastered medicine, conducted research into critical clinical issues of humans in space, and was now poised to fly in space. Along the way, I had learned one of the great lessons of success: if you want something badly enough and are willing to work hard, you can achieve it.

Since that time, I have gone on to do other things, pursue other professions, and achieve more accomplishments. That's been both wonderful and challenging. That's when I hit that tipping point where my drive to achieve became a need. It's akin to an addiction—one success is never enough. I needed more and even more after that. My sense of personal value was so closely tied to achievement that anything short of that recon-firmed internal doubts that I was not enough.

This is when I began to look deeper into myself. What were the motives, the origin of my drive to succeed? What are the "whys" that I mentioned in the previous chapter? Examining my upbringing and background told me all I needed to know to better understand myself. With the help of a counselor, I realized I didn't need to continue to strive to be better. I am good just the way I am.

Still, it is a shame that it has taken almost a lifetime to realize that I am enough. I've also learned that I am not alone in this discovery. There are many of us out there, including maybe even you reading this book.

The solution is to say to yourself that you are, in fact, enough. The recognition and acceptance of being imperfectly perfect let us all escape the exhausting treadmill of equating self-worth with perfection. As I said before, it's liberating. It's also inherently practical. At the risk of employing psychiatric terminology, it's a matter of emphasizing syntonic behavior as opposed to dystonic. Syntonic behavior is inherently constructive. It helps you move forward in life. It's consistent with your values. Dystonic behavior, on the other hand, is precisely the opposite. It's behavior that's destructive in nature, which goes against any sort of personal growth and development.

When you can tell yourself with sincerity that you are enough, you're engaging in syntonic behavior. When you accept your imperfect perfection, you're not just getting off your own back, but you're also working to improve your relationships with others and nurture an attitude founded on tolerance and acceptance—of your flawed self as well as others.

My personal journey has led me to this day and this book where I can openly discuss the positive and negative aspects of being "successful." I hope that in sharing my story, you can learn from me and the trials and tribulations of others to enrich your life.

KEEP AT IT

If you happen to be one of those people—perhaps I should say fortunate people—who are not subject to the disease that perfectionism can become, the solution might seem rather simple and straightforward. Just stop doing it. Stop beating yourself up over the absence of perfection. Stop making snap judgments about others. Stop inextricably connecting your sense of self-worth with the next success. To someone who doesn't have to deal with pursuing perfection, the answer seems obvious.

However, if you are, like me, one of those people who struggled with the pursuit of perfection, you know all too well it's not as simple as that.

Unshackling yourself from the bonds of perfectionism is very much a work in progress. You can't flip a switch and bid goodbye to coming down on yourself and others. It doesn't happen automatically.

Instead, moving away from the pursuit of perfection takes both time and commitment. It's important to be continually mindful, to watch for thoughts, attitudes, and actions that even hint at a critical, judgmental mindset with regard to both you and those around you.

That can be particularly challenging for younger people. As I discussed earlier, when we're young, we are naturally more attentive to achievement, success, and moving up in the world.

Anything that detracts from that focus can almost seem unnatural—as though you're unwilling or unable to keep up with everyone else.

To reiterate—that's not exclusively a bad thing. Youth is the time for the pursuit of significant life goals. But it never hurts to have a healthy perspective as you expend that kind of energy. Just because you're looking to achieve great things by no means mandates perfection. And the sooner you can recognize this—and understand it's a challenge you will have to confront repeatedly—not only will you be happier, but you'll also likely appreciate your successes more. Nothing has to be perfect to be worthwhile.

ACCEPTANCE

Coming to understand that chasing perfection can negatively impact your life can also offer another significant plus—applying the same guidelines to those around you.

I have had my share of relationships through the years. I have fallen in and out of love many times. And at each stage of life, how I love and my expectations from whom I love changed. Early in my life, love was locked on family, particularly my mother. She was my primary focus, trying to make her happy, particularly in my behavior as a kid. Later in my teenage years, I discovered girls. My focus then turned toward finding someone to love. As a young adult, it was identifying a person who loved me. (Does any of this sound familiar?)

Whether you are a man or a woman, we are all looking for The One. We are looking for someone who knows us and still loves us despite what they see. Many call it a soulmate. In some cases, a person saves us from the environment or from ourselves. Most relationships come with such baggage and expectations.

According to the book *The Soulmate Experience* by Mali Apple and Joe Dunn, a primary cause of issues with others arises when our expectations run counter to acceptance. Personal relationships are one such situation. The authors point out that, at the outset of a relationship, the object of our affection can do no wrong. You're accepting any flaws you see. It's like you're in a higher state of consciousness, one characterized by acceptance and an utter lack of judgment or criticism. As Apple and Dunn point out, "Being open and accepting is precisely what a higher state of consciousness is."

But, as we get to know that other person better, we gradually move toward less acceptance. Flaws suddenly become more obvious and certain character traits that we never noticed before suddenly set our teeth on edge. The reason, as Apple and Dunn note, is: "Our new partner falls off the pedestal not because we're suddenly seeing them realistically, but because we have gradually become less open to who they are." [7]

That's a powerful statement. When it comes to our expectations toward others, we should never let them overwhelm our capacity to embrace who they really are. Looked at another way, if you can observe yourself and your expectations with a realistic, nonjudgmental eye, do the same with those whom you care for. You'll both be much happier.

All of us are looking for someone to accept us for who we are and to love us unconditionally—the proverbial love "despite my warts." We want them committed to our relationship, to us above all others. But are these wants and desires truly realistic?

---

[7] Apple, Mali and Dunn, Joe, *The Soulmate Experience*, A Higher Possibility, 2011.

That's a somewhat unfortunate but nonetheless essential question you must ask yourself constantly throughout your life. We all want to be happy, but it can be dangerous to live under that veil of expectation.

Valerie always says that "Disappointments are a function of our expectation." That means we go into things with a set of expectations that fulfill what we want, need, and desire. But, if those things don't happen, disappointment ensues—disappointment with others as well as ourselves. When it comes to personal relationships, that can mean an awful lot of pressure, particularly when it involves people who are driven by perfection.

The solution is to accept others for who they are and not to expect perfection from them. If you're willing to give yourself a break and move away from the struggle to be perfect, grant those whom you care about the same opportunity. You'll be happier and much more likely headed down the path of meaningful, rewarding long relationships.

PERFECT IMPERFECTIONS

There is a song by John Legend entitled "All of Me." The lyrics contain a statement that is true of most relationships when we fall in love. Love allows us to accept the "perfect imperfections" of each other. As it happens, these words capture my current relationship with my former wife.

One of the main consequences of striving for perfection is that you not only see the faults of yourself but those of the people around you. When my ex-wife and I were dating, all I saw was her inherent beauty, kindness, and love for me. As we began to spend more time with each other, I began to see her imperfections. It was those issues that resulted in our eventual break-up. I saw her imperfections and they were incompatible with mine. Unfortunately, at that time, I did not have the tools to save our marriage.

With my partner now, we both recognize our incompatible shortcomings and are willing to work with each other. We resolve the ones we can and agree to disagree on the ones in dispute. We are learning to accept each other for who we are. We are both showing up differently than in our previous marriages, because we have grown as individuals.

In your relationships, if you can love someone enough to allow them to be exactly what they choose to be—without any expectations or attachments from you—you'll know true peace in your lifetime. True love means you love a person for what they are, not for what you think they should be. This is an open mind and an absence of attachment to the outcomes.

That means more than just accepting others' imperfections. It also means accepting your own. However, we may strive to achieve and grow; none of us are perfect nor will we ever be. In fact, truly believing in yourself includes this acceptance that we can all strive to achieve and be the very best we can be, while embracing our underlying flaws and imperfections.

As astronaut John Glenn put it as he prepared to step into history as the first American in space: "As I sat, strapped in my seat waiting during the countdown, one thought kept crossing my mind…every part of this rocket was supplied by the lowest bidder."

Flawed? Yes. Still, a resounding success? Without a doubt.

CHAPTER 9

YOU ARE A CHILD OF GOD

....

*"I am divinity defined, I am the God on the
Inside, I am a star, a piece of it all, I am light."*
—India Arie, "I Am Light"

....

The greatest epiphany I've ever had in my life occurred when I discovered my place in the universe.

This doesn't specifically refer to my work as an astronaut and the privilege and experience of taking part in a spacewalk, although it was an important waypoint in the journey. Rather, I identified my place in the grand scheme of things by establishing my connection to the power of the universe.

I refer here to God.

Most religions have their foundation in a spiritual leader who could tap into this infinite knowledge, transforming it into actions and words for their followers. When I was in college, I studied many of the major religions to understand faith and belief and their place in my life.

According to some estimates, there are twenty-one formal religions worldwide, with followers scattered around the globe. For many believers, religion plays an essential role in influencing all aspects of their daily life. The largest religions in the world generally belong to one of the two main subgroups. These are the Abrahamic religions (Islam, Christianity, Judaism, Baha'i, and so on) and the Indian religions (Hinduism, Buddhism, Sikhism, Jainism, and so forth). This is based on the Pew Research Institute and other international demographic databases.[8]

My study of these different religions affirmed that Christianity was right for me. After all, it was the faith of my family—an integral part of my life. But I had to seek and choose for myself. It may prove helpful to you to choose and study on your own. This is an individual exercise. Like myself, you will find that, first, religion is a human-made phenomena and construct. Second, all roads lead to spiritual enlightenment and a higher consciousness.

One of my favorite passages in the King James Version of the Bible is in Romans 8:1–25 as it discusses "Deliverance from Bondage":

> There is therefore now no condemnation for those who are in Christ Jesus. For the law of the spirit of life in Christ Jesus has set you free from the law of sin and of death. For the mind set on the flesh is death, but the mind set on the spirit is life and peace.

It then goes on to say that the universe is seeking those children of God.

---

[8]   "Top 10 Largest Religions in the World in 2024," The Countries Of, https://thecountriesof.com/largest-religions-in-the-world/.

My ultimate goal in life is to seek to be Christ-like. By that, I mean working to obtain the peace and power that Jesus Christ demonstrated in the Bible. The reality is that He was not the only one. History is filled with men and women who have found enlightenment, although, in my opinion, none of the magnitude of Jesus. I believe these individuals come into this world to show us the truth and the way to the infinite. So, whether you are Christian or not, it is important that you take on your journey of self-discovery of who you really are. As I like to phrase it, be "an Infinite Being with infinite possibilities."

Naturally, I'm far from the only person who has been fortunate enough to recognize this connection; I'm just one of many throughout the history of mankind. Moses and John the Baptist are two such people mentioned in the Bible. Philosophers—often a hard-baked bunch when it comes to matters of faith—include such noteworthy names as Richard Swinburne of Oxford University who have professed his belief in God. Writers—yet another group prone to skepticism—offer C.S. Lewis, Leo Tolstoy, and any number of other luminaries. All these people and others made this discovery in their own way—a journey that I feel we should all undertake at some time in our lives.

Then there are scientists—perhaps the most noteworthy include Albert Einstein and Francis Bacon—who recognized the presence of God. That raises a particularly prickly question, at least in the minds of some. As one woman asked me after I spoke at an event: "How can you, as a scientist, believe in God?"

My answer, which may surprise you, is straightforward: "I believe in the existence of God because I exist."

As you look around at this miracle of life, you see plants and animals in their places, mountains and oceans teeming with life of all forms. At the cellular and genetic level, molecules and atoms behave according to laws that enable life. I realized early in my science studies that, despite all the laws that make up our understanding of the world, humankind is not actually responsible for the creation of those laws. We only describe things that are already there.

Laws of thermodynamics, Newton's law, electromagnetism, and even gravity are simply words given to things that already exist. We didn't create a thing in this world as we know it. And, so far as those inventions and innovations that we lay claim to, their foundation derives from the material and substrate that were already here. As we learn more about the natural elements and inner workings of this universe, we are, at best, co-creators.

That's why I believe God exists. I see God all around me every day as definitive evidence of one power and one source of all things. Accordingly, one of my favorite prayers is: "The light of God surrounds me; the love of God enfolds me; the power of God protects me; the presence of God watches over me." This means that we move in and out God simply by our mere existence in this universe.

Another favorite is the prayer from Romans 8:19 (King James version): "The anxious longing of the creation waits eagerly for the revealing of the Sons, (and I added "Daughters") of God." So, our path through life is to gradually gain knowledge and experience in order to unfold our true nature. This may take a lifetime to accomplish.

For me, the existence of God is evident. God exists in us and everything that surrounds us. People come to this discovery through different means, which is as it should be. But for me, all I have to do is take a good look around at our world to be completely convinced of this truth.

THE CHRIST WITHIN

Since I first accepted God and Christ as the spiritual path that I would walk, I have believed that we are all children of God. There is something inherent in all of us that connects us to something greater than ourselves. There is a living force that binds us, an intelligence that guides us even if we are not believers. I have friends who are atheists, who believe just the opposite. They feel there are no higher powers, and we simply exist in the world as biological beings at the whim of the forces of natural laws. They believe that our lives are the result of the actions we take. I have been in plenty of arguments about the facts on both sides. Truth be told, I believe in all those things, too. My belief allows both to be true at the same time. Ultimately, it comes down to what you believe and what works for you.

My belief is that Jesus Christ came into this world to show us the way. Whether He is the son of God or not, most would acknowledge that out of all the "prophets," He has had a tremendous impact on our civilization. His teachings and simply His nature illustrated a way of life that has brought peace to many and highlighted the path toward enlightenment. I believe that we can become Christ-like, that we are all Christ in our own way. We are imbued with the same powers that He demonstrated during His brief time on Earth. Jesus Christ's real power came from self-realization and self-actualization that we all have unique gifts and talents to share with the world, the discovery of which comes from our connection to the one true power of God. There is an intelligence in the universe that surrounds us and envelopes us. In fact, it is made up of all the things around us. All the things we see is part of this universal power or force that I call "God." I am convinced that if we choose, we can obtain the same powers for good.

This force, by its nature, is neutral, neither good nor bad. It only becomes good or bad by the consciousness that directs its actions. Said a different way, you and I can determine how this force is exhibited. Here lies the foundation of the concept of good and evil, of God and the Devil. Many religions, including Christianity and Islam, have been built on this premise. At the heart of both religions is the desire to promote good moral judgment and action. They teach us how to live better and fulfilling lives. I wish that all religions could focus on that and not on our differences.

DISCOVERING YOUR TRUE NATURE

The recognition of God is an essential step to a topic that this book has covered from the very first few pages—the importance of discovering your true self and where you belong in the universe.

For one thing, if you share my perspective on God, it can be something of a humbling experience. The recognition that everything that surrounds us here on Earth is not exclusively of our own making can prove a healthy jolt against human hubris. Again, we don't necessarily create; we merely attach labels in most cases.

But, regarding finding your true nature, a belief in the existence of God can prove to be a healthy guidepost on your journey to self-discovery and awareness. Phrased simply: Since God exists, where do you fit in? Where is your true place in a universe that God has fashioned for you?

Here, God can serve as a valuable role model. Although none of us can hope to be God, we can bend our efforts to being more like God whenever possible. Leveraging happiness as well as challenges, tragedies, and disappointment, we can use the example of God as a launchpad for growth in every aspect of our lives.

Again, too, this is not about chasing perfection (we learned all about the perils of that in an earlier chapter.) Rather, it's a recognition that we are all perfectly imperfect, flaws and all, who should work ceaselessly to make our lives and those around us better.

Two biblical verses come to mind pertaining to this:

> "Not that I have already obtained all this, or have already arrived at my goal, but I press on to take hold of that for which Christ Jesus took hold of me." —Philippians 3:12 (King James version)

> "Brethren, I do not regard myself as having laid hold of it yet; One thing I do: Forgetting What lies behind and reaching forward to what lies ahead, press on toward the goal for the prize of the upward call of God in Christ Jesus." —Philippians 4:12–14

The journey toward being God-like is not insignificant. Working to discover our true selves and our best role in the order of things doesn't make us just one of countless others. Rather, by striving for greater understanding and acceptance—both of ourselves and others—we reinforce our individual significance and meaning. As Persian poet Rumi pointed out: "You are not a drop in the ocean but the entire ocean in a drop."[9] We are always looking outside of ourselves for meaning, when the truth is that the answers we seek are already with us. We must take the time

---

[9]   Rumi, Jalāl al-Dīn Muhammad, Rumi Center for Spirituality and the Arts.

to uncover that. In this discovery, we realize that we are vast and complex in nature, capable of unlimited growth.

THE IMPORTANCE OF SETTING PRIORITIES

The search for one's true self may seem highly abstract and largely dependent on individual needs and circumstances. In many ways, it is. In my case, in addition to a good deal of soul searching, I've studied a number of religions and read a variety of self-help books, authors, and philosophers. The result of all this study has led me to compile a set of priorities and mindsets to direct my daily actions and reactions to the challenges and opportunities that life presents.

When I went to college, it wasn't only to become a pre-med student striving to be a doctor one day, it was also to find myself. I have always been curious about the origin of life. One of my goals during this period was to learn as much as I could about humanity through the study of religion, philosophy, and science. So, I read as much as I could about great thought leaders on the subject. My range of interests went from the study of the Bible, the Koran, Hinduism, and others, to astronomy and astrophysics. This became the foundation on which I set my life's priorities.

I found this to be particularly helpful in keeping me focused on goals that I hope to achieve as my journey continues. Now my daily practice includes meditation and affirmations that further strengthen my focus—perhaps you may find some of them beneficial as well. With this in mind, I submit the following construct with the assistance of a number of authors.

Enlightenment. This is truly at the core of my journey of self-discovery. This includes an ongoing emphasis on mindfulness as well as steps to grow what I refer to as my "spiritual capital." The overall effort is geared toward aligning my consciousness with both the presence and the power of God.

There are several stories about people who have become enlightened. The most famous is Jesus Christ. If you believe in the Bible, He was born to become the salvation of the world. His journey took him from a stable to the height of spiritual power. His life became the roadmap toward enlightenment for followers through the ages.

Buddha is another who went from an upper-class life to become a humble servant of the people and God. Both journeys tell the story of how to become enlightened no matter your station in life—the ultimate human goal.

Expanding Consciousness. This, too, is at the heart of self-discovery. Implicit in the journey to self-understanding is an overall growth of consciousness, incorporating mind, body, and spirit. Like enlightenment, an expanded consciousness emphasizes development of mindfulness to boost awareness of and connection with the moment.

At the heart of enlightenment is the expansion of consciousness. By definition, the elevation of one's consciousness is required. Defining it is important. At its core, consciousness is simply awareness of yourself in context to your surroundings. Awareness of your place in the universe makes you unique, as does your place in it.

In my studies, I discovered there are different levels of consciousness. Sigmund Freud, the father of psychology, is well-known for his psychological levels of consciousness. His model of the conscious, preconscious, and unconscious mind is generally agreed upon today as:

1. The Preconscious—The preconscious is a place where most of our memory is stored. It is composed of all the information that we could potentially bring forward into the conscious mind if we chose to do so.

2. The Conscious—The conscious level of awareness is a place where we can logically and rationally analyze and discuss the vastness of our memories, feelings, and desires in any given moment. It is an aspect of our thought process where we find ourselves distinctly aware of both internal and external influences.

3. The Unconscious—The unconscious mind is a place where all memory is kept, whether or not we are presently aware of its existence. Often, it is a mental storehouse where we "lock away" our more unpleasant feelings, memories, and urges. Still, the unconscious mind is still thought to have a major influence on our overall behavior.[10]

From a spiritual perspective, there are three levels of consciousness: simple consciousness, self-consciousness, and cosmic consciousness. The levels of consciousness

---

[10] Diaz, Cheyenne, "Levels of Consciousness: Expand Your View of the Universe," Mindvalley Blog, 2018.

described by Freud is embodied in simple and self-consciousness. The ultimate goal of true believers is the attainment of cosmic consciousness. The following is an excerpt from *Cosmic Consciousness* by Richard Maurice Bucke:

> It must be clearly understood that all cases of Cosmic Consciousness are not on the same plane. Or, if we speak of Simple Consciousness, Self-Consciousness and Cosmic Consciousness as each occupying a plane, then, as the range of Self Consciousness on its plane (where one man may be an Aristotle, a Cæsar, a Newton, or a Comte, while his neighbor on the next street may be intellectually and morally, to all appearance, little if at all above the animal in his stable) is far greater than the range of Simple Consciousness in any given species on its plane, so we must suppose that the range of Cosmic Consciousness (given millions of cases, as on the other planes) is greater than that of Self Consciousness, and it probably is in fact very much greater both in kind and degree: that is to say, given a world peopled with men having Cosmic Consciousness, they would vary both in the way of greater and less intellectual ability, and greater and less moral and spiritual elevation, and also in the

way of variety of character, more than would the inhabitants of a planet on the plane of Self Consciousness. Within the plane of Cosmic Consciousness one man shall be a god while another shall not be, to casual observation, lifted so very much above ordinary humanity, however much his inward life may be exalted, strengthened and purified by the new sense. But, as the Self-Conscious man (however degraded) is in fact almost infinitely above the animal with merely simple consciousness, so any man permanently endowed with the Cosmic Sense would be almost infinitely higher and nobler than any man who is Self-Conscious merely. And not only so, but the man who has had the Cosmic Sense for even a few moments only will probably never again descend to the spiritual level of the merely self-conscious man, but twenty, thirty or forty years afterwards he will still feel within him the purifying, strengthening and exalting effect of that divine illumination, and many of those about him will recognize that his spiritual stature is above that of the average man.[11]

---

[11]   Burke, Richard Maurice, *Cosmic Consciousness*, Innes and Sons, 1905, p. 56.

In other words, to transcend to cosmic consciousness, you must advance through simple and self-consciousness. I believe that enlightenment leads to a higher consciousness, and this enables cosmic consciousness.

> "Who looks outside, dreams;
> who looks inside, awakes."
> —CARL JUNG

LETTING GO OF FEAR

This is a critical step on the road to personal growth and self-discovery. By releasing fear, you're inherently embracing possibilities and opportunities. Nor is it just a matter of shedding needless hurdles or limiting beliefs. By letting go of fear, you become that much more accepting of others as they are—an important component of self-discovery. My focus these days is to free myself from worry, anxiety, and regret. In addition to letting go of fear, I am also letting go of criticizing and judging others.

> "I learned that courage was not the
> absence of fear, but the triumph over it."
> —NELSON MANDELA

In 1993, as I sat on top the Space Shuttle Columbia (STS-55), I was understandably nervous about launching into space. My crew and I waited for launch control to complete their pre-flight checks. At T minus two minutes, we were asked to "close visors and start O2." At this point, I closed and locked my helmet visor and flipped a switch to turn on the oxygen in my space suit. By now I was really nervous. At T minus five seconds, the main engines of Columbia roared to life, and we could feel every pound of the 1.5 million pounds of thrust. Just a few moments later, however, there was another sound, one of alarm, indicating that a malfunction had occurred in one of our three engines. Suddenly there was silence as Commander Steve Nagel turned off the alarm. We were safe! Or so I thought. As I instinctively used my wrist mirror to look out the overhead windows of the flight deck, I could see smoke rolling up the side of the shuttle. I thought for a moment that it was over for me and all of us on the shuttle that day.

Fortunately, NASA had gone through that a few years earlier. We became the second shuttle flight to experience a "launch pad abort." After an hour or so, after ensuring the safety of the shuttle, we were asked to leave it, to fly another day.

This experience gave me a better appreciation for life. It reminded me how lucky we were to live, with an opportunity to fly another day. And when that day came a month later, I needed to push down the apprehension and fear of climbing into that same ship once again. If I had not done so, I would have been literally grounded here on Earth and my dream of flying in space would be lost. I would have never experienced the beauty and grandeur of our planet from God's eye view. To accomplish my dream, I let go of fear and embraced my future. It would have been a dream deferred.

Langston Hughes, a 20th century poet wrote a poem called "Harlem" that has always stuck with me. It described in words the consequences of a dream deferred. If it was within my power,

I wasn't going to let anything, keep me from accomplishing my dream.[12]

EMBRACING LIFE

My experience encapsulates many of the individual parts of self-discovery I've already pointed out. Mindfulness, living in the moment, releasing fear, and embracing the presence and power of God come together to a life that's built on love, compassion for others, and the courage to pursue self-knowledge and understanding of your place in the universe. Focusing on this can lead to a life that encompasses much more than a litany of common, even hollow experiences. Maya Angelou said it best: "Life is not measured by the number of breaths you take but by the moments that take your breath away."

Embracing life and all it has to offer helps us discover the meaning of our life. It helps us set goals that lead to a life fulfilled.

A significant part of life is finding love—love for ourselves and others, whether a spouse, a family, or vocation. I am a big movie buff; I love science fiction movies, particularly about space. They capture my imagination and help me project the possibilities of our universe. Imagine my surprise when in the middle of the movie *Interstellar*, with Matthew McConaughey and Anne Hathaway, there was a line about love: "Love is the one thing that we are capable of perceiving that transcends dimensions of time and space. Maybe we should trust that even if we can't understand it."

---

[12]   Hughes, Langston, "Harlem," The Collected Works of Langston Hughes, Harold Ober Associates Inc., 1990.

The message that I received was the importance of love, even though we do not really understand it. It is a critical part of life. If we are lucky to find it, we must hold on to it, despite not knowing where it comes from. When it happens, it just is. We should let go and embrace it. In many cases, it could bring additional joy into our lives.

I have a dear friend who was diagnosed with a chronic disease called parkinsonism. It is characterized by tremor, bradykinesia (slow movements), rigidity, and postural instability. Parkinsonism robs you of your ability to function normally and, for many, it can be debilitating. When they were first diagnosed, they were in denial for four years until the physical signs couldn't be ignored. Later, after receiving treatment, they didn't tell any of their family members for fear that they couldn't handle the diagnosis and would be treated differently. After ten years, their fears were realized. Despite having this disease, my friend has faced it head on, not letting it keep them from living their life. In fact, for them it has done quite the opposite. They are continuing to live a full life. When asked "How?" They responded, "If Parkinson gets the best of me, I want to make sure that I live my best life."

They continue to amaze me with their strength and positive attitude in the midst of this disease. They have embraced life in all that it has to offer. A lesson for us all.

FINDING YOUR MISSION

As an astronaut, I am well acquainted with the true meaning of the term "mission."

When anyone refers to traveling in space, it's not as though they're taking some sort of improvised trip. It is a mission and everything that entails must be considered—why you're going into space, what you intend to do, how you intend to return, and what you hope to learn as a result of a successful mission.

Those are guidelines that we would do well to follow in our own mission to discover who we are, what our place is on Earth and in the universe, and what we can realistically hope to achieve. By setting out those parameters, like an astronaut blasting into space, you can embark on a meaningful journey with the confidence that careful planning and foresight can offer. You know precisely where you wish to go, how you're going to get there, and, perhaps most significantly, what your journey means.

My own mission includes:

- I want to be a man who puts God first in everything.
- I want to be a man who sets big, hairy, audacious goals (BHAG) in life and strives to accomplish them.
- I want to be a man who is a leader, provider, caregiver, mentor, fearless, risk-taker, faithful, devoted, lover, husband, and father.
- I want to be a man who takes his God-given talents to create opportunities that positively change lives, including family, others, and his own.
- I want to be a man whose goal is to build wealth—wealth defined as building significant resources spiritually, psychologically, physically, emotionally, and financially.

My mission has a common goal: to make a real difference in the world, to leverage those resources and that wealth brings for Good and for God. What is yours?

I began this book by mentioning how my view of the universe was greatly impacted by the perspective afforded by my spacewalk. Here is an excerpt from my first book:

February 9, 1995 – Michael and I were nearing the end of our EVA. While he wrapped up a few final details, I had been given the extraordinary opportunity to relax during our last full day and night pass, leisurely dangling from the robotic arm, about thirty-five feet above the payload bay, my mind floating as freely and unencumbered as my body. I gazed down fondly at my fellow crew members inside the ship. Behind them was the seemingly enormous planet Earth, a welcoming blue-green orb dotted with fleecy clouds. Still further beyond, it seemed I could see the whole universe, billions of stars and planets infinitely receding into the blackness. As you might imagine, in that moment I felt extremely small in the grand scheme of things.

But then, while pondering all of my own insignificance, I started to remember how far I had come, from being one small boy among millions, lying on my back gazing up at the stars, to being one of only 350 human beings who had ever flown in space, to one of 50 who had ever walked in space, to one of only 15 African Americans who had traveled in space, to one single African American, the only one who would ever be the first, to walk in space.... And on that day, at that moment, in my mind I became larger than life. The past and future became the present, and I was one with the universe.

> We are multi-potential beings with unlimited
> power to become anything we desire.

Although you're likely never going to have a similar experience in terms of the actual location, that doesn't mean you can't develop a similar expansive viewpoint. All it takes is a step outside your own "capsule" and, from there, a careful, attentive look around. Even though your feet may be firmly on the ground, it's how you can begin to connect to being one with the universe.

You are a divine being with extraordinary power. You are capable of anything that you set your mind to do.

THE WAKE-UP CALL

The Covid-19 pandemic changed the world. It made us stop and think about our place in the world. For many of us, we now look at life differently. In 2020, the world lost over 3 million people, according to the World Health Organization. No one knows the actual number because of the difficulty in reporting. A third of those deaths were in the United States. With all this illness and death around us, we could not help but be impacted by it. I lost several friends and family to Covid-19. It placed us all in a state of fear. I believe it will take us years to recover, especially for our youth. The effect on the educational system is far-reaching!

The pandemic brought us closer together as a nation and world in certain respects and tore us apart in other ways. For me, it transformed my thinking about me and my place in the world. When faced with death, we are forced to choose life, to find the truth in others and in ourselves. This kind of event raises our consciousness and increases our compassion.

Toward the end of the pandemic, I suffered a mini-stoke, called a transient ischemic attack. I was standing in the kitchen putting away the groceries and talking with Valerie when I suddenly lost the use of my left arm and my ability to speak. She immediately helped me to the floor where I stayed until the ambulance arrived. While on the floor, I had plenty of time to think about my perceived short life. I was thinking, even though I had trouble speaking, about my life and the people that I had met, and the people that I was possibly leaving behind, especially my daughter. Would I get a chance to say goodbye? What would become of her? How would she react to me being gone or left with a chronic debilitating state? Fortunately, I had family with me. At least I wasn't alone. It was very scary to say the least.

I was fortunate to have gotten fast and responsive care from the EMS team and the hospital. It turned out that the local hospital specializes in stroke care. Within a few days, I made a full physical recovery. But I was mentally slower than usual. (That's a joke.) I was blessed in many ways, because things could have been different. Today I am fully recovered and active.

This event made me reconsider a lot of things in my life. The superman that I thought I was had a weakness, a kryptonite, which reminded me that I was human and frail. I began to not take life so seriously. Letting go of things was the hardest thing that I had to do. Sometimes God sends you a wake-up call, an opportunity to reset your priorities in life to what is important.

I began to let go of things, like my job, my business, my need for order, and my worries. I am actively trying to do things differently, being more mindful and intentional about life.

In retrospect, I have been so focused on achieving that I didn't take the time to live life to its fullest. Let me explain. When you look at what I have accomplished, there is no doubt that I have had a blessed life. I have traveled the world, in and above the atmosphere. I have experienced different cultures, and have, in fact, lived and visited other countries. I have gotten to know the best and worst of society and its people. By all definition, I have lived a full life.

But I haven't explored deeply enough myself. I have been defining myself through my experiences and not truly experiencing life. My thoughts in the past have always been what's next and not what's now. Living in the present is now my ultimate goal. It's letting go of the little things and focusing on the loving things. If we could all do this, the world would be in a better place than it is today.

The hope of my book is that you will take the insights, lessons, experiences, and openness to help you achieve an honest and fulfilling life, too.

INFINITE BEING WITH INFINITE POSSIBILITIES

We are infinite beings with infinite possibilities. It is worth repeating that we are multipotential, multi-talented, and born for a reason. There are no accidents of birth. We are capable of doing great things in life. We are only limited by our ability to see ourselves as the infinite creatures we are. Part of this infiniteness is our ability to tap into the one source of power that drives the universe. There are forces bigger than ourselves that are all around us and through us. It is in us and surrounds and enables our existence. It lies in the air we breathe, it is everywhere, from to the gravity that holds us to the surface of this planet, to the forces that hold our solar system and galaxy together, and the billions of galaxies that make up the universe as we know it.

The plain truth is that we each have a role to play in the cosmic dance. Our talents are added to the music of the grand orchestra of life. Have you ever listened to a band or orchestra? Even though you can hear distinct instruments, it is the coordination of the different instruments and notes that make music. It's magical. It is that music that touches the hearts of all those who are truly listening. Our goal should be to learn to play our instrument as best as we can, so we can add it to the symphony of existence. We can participate in our own way, utilizing our talents for the edification of ourselves and the world around us. We have great potential if we only recognize it.

Our job is to live up to the potential that God has trusted us to do. Remember that we are children of the universe, imbued with that same power. There is nothing we cannot do once we recognize this truth.

APPENDIX

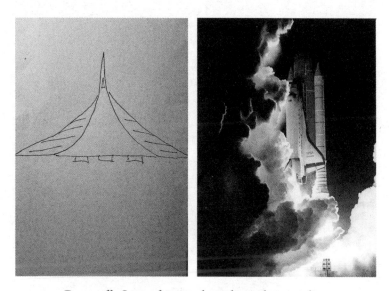

Bernard's Spaceship in the 7th grade vs reality

ACKNOWLEDGMENTS

In *Dream Walker: A Journey of Achievement and Inspiration*, I took the opportunity to thank many of the people who have contributed to my life up to that point. This was more than ten years ago! I have had many more blessings since then. Much is owed to the people in my life and God.

My daughter is all grown up now. After graduating from Texas Tech University in psychology and business, she went on to accept a job with one of the top companies in the world. She is a wonderful soul whom I greatly admire and is my greatest accomplishment in life. I am so proud of the person she has become.

I fell in love with a wonderful woman a few years after a difficult divorce. In fact, we both survived the trauma that divorce can have on people. We are committed partners in love and friendship. I am truly beholden to Valerie Mosley for being in my life to this day, supporting me, listening to me, and simply being there as a friend.

Since my last book, I lost one of the stewards of my life, my mother, to Alzheimer's disease. It was painful to watch this devastating disease rob her of her mind, taking the things that she treasured—her order, structure, and discipline. She lost these attributes that she harnessed over the years to become a dedicated teacher, committed wife, and loving mother. I thank her for passing those traits onto me. I also recently lost Joe Burgess, my stepfather, who showed me how to be a man and a devoted husband, which he was to my mother for forty-eight years.

I have had two great bosses who have managed my life and me: Tamara Vaugh, my executive assistant while I was at the National Math and Science Initiative, and Pamela Jones, COO of Vesalius Ventures. Pam continues to be one of my good friends and colleagues in her new journey running her own business. I owe them both a debt of gratitude.

Also, I would like to thank my sister and brother and family and my friends who have stuck by me through the years. As we are all getting older now, our conversations sound more and more like our parents—"What are the kids doing or not doing?"—and taking time to count our blessings each and every day. I am truly blessed to have them in my life.

Lastly, I want to acknowledge Ed Dwight, sculptoy, retired Captain in the US Air Force, and first African American Astronaut Candidate in the 1960's, who never got an opportunity to fly into space. I thank him for opening the door for me. On May 19, 2024, he fulfilled his dream to become the oldest astronaut to fly into space on Blue Origin spacecraft. He is an inspiration for us all.

I finalized the writing of this book with the assistance of my friend Jeff Wuorio, in one of our favorite places in the world: Healdsburg, California, in the heart of Sonoma wine country. It is one of the most spiritual places in the world. It is my happy place; it's where I receive spiritual power and energy. I cannot think of a better place to have written a book on embracing the infinite possibilities of life.

Retired Captain Ed Dwight, surrounded by
NASA Astronauts: Charlie Bolden, Leland
Melvin, Bernard Harris and Victor Glover